THE GREAT
HISPANIC HERITAGE

Carlos Santana

THE GREAT HISPANIC HERITAGE

THE GREAT
HISPANIC HERITAGE

Carlos Santana

Louise Chipley Slavicek

CHELSEA HOUSE
PUBLISHERS
An imprint of Infobase Publishing

Carlos Santana

Copyright © 2006 by Infobase Publishing

All rights reserved. No part of this book may be reproduced or utilized in any form or by any means, electronic or mechanical, including photocopying, recording, or by any information storage or retrieval systems, without permission in writing from the publisher. For information contact:

Chelsea House
An imprint of Infobase Publishing
132 West 31st Street
New York NY 10001

ISBN-10: 0-7910-8844-8
ISBN-13: 978-0-7910-8844-9

Library of Congress Cataloging-in-Publication Data
Slavicek, Louise Chipley, 1956–
    Carlos Santana / Louise Chipley Slavicek.
       p. cm. — (Great Hispanic heritage)
    Includes bibliographical references and index.
    ISBN 0-7910-8844-8 (hard cover)
    1. Santana, Carlos—Juvenile literature. 2. Rock musicians—United States—
Bibliography—Juvenile literature. I. Title. III. Series.
    ML3930.S26.S53 2005
    787.87'164092—dc22   2005026000

Chelsea House books are available at special discounts when purchased in bulk quantities for business, associations, institutions, or sales promotions. Please call our Special Sales Department in New York at (212) 967-8800 or (800) 322-8755.

You can find Chelsea House on the World Wide Web at http://www.chelseahouse.com

Series design by Terry Mallon
Cover design by Keith Trego

Printed in the United States of America

Bang EJB 10 9 8 7 6 5 4 3 2

This book is printed on acid-free paper.

All links and web addresses were checked and verified to be correct at the time of publication. Because of the dynamic nature of the web, some addresses and links may have changed since publication and may no longer be valid.

Table of Contents

Humanitarian and Superstar

On the evening of August 30, 2004, some of the entertainment world's brightest stars, including singer Rob Thomas, actress Salma Hayek, and comedian George Lopez, gathered at the Century Plaza Hotel in Los Angeles. They had come to pay homage to one of the most celebrated and influential Hispanics of their era: Carlos Santana. That night, the Mexican-American guitarist and songwriter was honored as the Latin Academy of Recording Arts and Sciences Person of the Year.

By almost any standards, Carlos Santana's long musical career has been extraordinary. In 1969, Santana and the multiracial, self-named band he helped found stunned the rock world with their electrifying performance at the famed Woodstock Music and Art Fair. Since his show-stopping appearance at Woodstock, Carlos Santana has sold more than 80 million albums with his band and as a solo artist, played live to upwards of 40 million fans on six

On August 30, 2004, Carlos Santana was named the Latin Academy of Recording Arts and Sciences Person of the Year for his musical and philanthropic contributions. The Mexican-American songwriter/guitarist is pictured here during the awards ceremony at the Century Plaza Hotel in Los Angeles, with his wife, Deborah, and his eldest son, Salvador.

continents, and won dozens of awards and honors, including ten Grammys and three Latin Grammys.

"PROGRESS, NOT SUCCESS"

Yet, it was not merely Carlos Santana's impressive accomplishments as a musician that the Latin Academy wanted to commemorate that August evening in Los Angeles. In choosing him as its Person of the Year, the Academy was also paying tribute to Carlos Santana's outstanding humanitarian achievements. In 1998, Carlos and his wife of more than 30 years, Deborah King Santana, founded the Milagro Foundation to assist underprivileged children and teenagers around the globe in the areas of education, health, and the arts. (Milagro is Spanish for "miracle.") Almost entirely funded by the Santanas, since its creation the Milagro Foundation has provided more than $2 million to agencies and charities in dozens of countries. In recent years, the couple have also donated millions of dollars to a host of other charitable and political action organizations, including Doctors Without Borders, Save the Children, Greenpeace, the Rainforest Action Network, Amnesty International, and various groups devoted to fighting the AIDS pandemic in Africa.

When the Chicano guitarist and songwriter finally took the stage on the evening of August 30, 2004, it was, characteristically, his humanitarian efforts and aims that he wanted to talk about rather than his numerous career triumphs. "My agenda is unifying the collective consciousness of the world," the soft-spoken musician told his listeners. "If I could establish one thing before I die, it would be to plant seeds of a vision that everyone all over the world would have water, electricity, food, and education for free."[1] Santana admitted that his dream was a bold one. Yet it was also attainable, he insisted. If people of all nations would only commit themselves to sharing the globe's available resources, he declared, his goal of eradicating hunger, poverty, and ignorance throughout the world could be realized within a span of two or three decades. "I'm into progress, not success," Santana recently explained to an interviewer. "Success is one beautiful cake. You cut it and you eat it yourself, and you choke on it. Progress, you cut it and you feed people with it, and hopefully you save a little piece for yourself. That's where I'm coming from."[2]

"To Make a Difference in the World"
There can be little doubt that Carlos Santana's determination

to help the disadvantaged peoples—and particularly the needy children—of the world is closely linked to his own experiences growing up in Mexico and in San Francisco's predominantly Hispanic Mission District. The middle of seven children, Carlos spent his earliest years in the impoverished farming village of Autlán de Navarro, where modern conveniences like electricity, running water, and indoor plumbing were not part of everyday life. After the Santanas moved to the squalid border town of Tijuana in 1955, eight-year-old Carlos worked as a street musician, playing traditional Mexican ballads for the American *turistas* for 50 cents a song to help support his family. By the time he was 13, Carlos was playing guitar seven nights a week in the house band of a strip joint on Tijuana's seedy main drag. When Carlos was 15, the Santanas left their Mexican homeland for San Francisco in search of a better life for themselves and their children. Yet even in their American "Promised Land," the new immigrants found themselves struggling just to get by financially. To ensure that there would always be enough food on the family's table, Carlos worked after school as a dishwasher and performed with local rock bands on weekend evenings.

In 1967, 19-year-old Carlos finally quit his day job to devote himself to his fledgling music career and the self-named band he had recently founded with several other Bay Area musicians. Santana's unique blend of Latin, jazz, blues, and rock music quickly brought the group a large and devoted following in San Francisco. In 1969, the up-and-coming band won both a major record contract and a chance to perform at the most publicized rock-and-roll event of the decade: the Woodstock Music and Art Fair in Bethel, New York. By the early 1970s, with three best-selling and critically acclaimed albums and a slew of Latin-fired hit singles to their credit, Carlos and his young bandmates had become international superstars.

Despite—or perhaps because of—Santana's meteoric rise to the top of the rock world, however, the band began to

During the 42nd Annual Grammy Awards in February 2000, Santana was honored eight times for his 1999 album *Supernatural*. In addition to winning Album of the Year, Santana's salsa-tinged song with Rob Thomas, "Smooth," earned him Record of the Year.

disintegrate soon after the release of its third album. Fed up with the constant bickering and internal power struggles, by 1973 Carlos had officially taken over the group that bore his name. As Santana moved his band in a more jazzy and spiritual direction over the next two decades, the group would undergo repeated personnel changes, as well as many commercial ups and downs.

After years of modest record sales, Santana hit a remarkable resurrection in 1999, following the release of the CD *Supernatural*. Featuring a host of popular and talented young guest artists, such as Rob Thomas and Lauryn Hill, the album eventually sold more than 25 million copies worldwide and earned a slew of Grammys. The phenomenally successful *Supernatural* and its follow-up CD *Shamen* introduced Carlos' Latin-spiked concoction of rock, blues, and jazz to a brand-new generation of fans. They would also make the guitarist wealthier and more famous than he had ever been before.

Yet as 57-year-old Carlos Santana prepared to accept his award as the Latin Academy's Person of the Year for 2004, it was evident that the Latino superstar had little interest in the spoils fame provides. Instead, he is committed to using his fame, wealth, and music to help his less fortunate brothers and sisters around the globe and convey a message of compassion and unity to all his listeners. "It's a glorious time for me and my wife," Santana confided to *Hispanic* magazine shortly before the awards ceremony. "I feel very grateful that we can do things that can make a difference in the world."[3]

Carlos Santana's Musical Heritage

Early in the morning of July 20, 1947, in the small Mexican village of Autlán de Navarro, José Santana and Josefina Barragán welcomed their fourth child and second son into the world. From the beginning, Carlos, as José and Josefina named the infant, stood out. In the social hierarchy of mid-twentieth-century Mexico, a fair complexion was viewed as a sign of God's favor and Carlos' skin tone was noticeably lighter than that of his siblings. On seeing him for the first time, the newborn's aunt declared that little Carlos was "*cristalino*: someone who would make his mark in the world."[4]

AUTLÁN DE NAVARRO: A PLACE OUT OF TIME

Nestled in a picturesque valley encircled by the Sierra Madre, Carlos Santana's birthplace is in the west-central Mexican state of Jalisco, about one hundred miles southwest of Guadalajara, the state capital. In Náhuatl, the native language of central Mexico, the word

Autlán means a place where there is a water route or canal. The remote Indian village was conquered by the Spanish in 1524, three years after the famed conquistador Hernán Cortés captured Tenochtitlán (modern-day Mexico City) and overthrew the mighty Aztec Empire.

In 1947, when Carlos Santana was born, only a few thousand people lived in Autlán de Navarro. Compared with Mexico City and the country's other major cities, Autlán appeared to belong to another time. There was no electricity, no running water, and no indoor plumbing. Roads were unpaved and chickens roamed freely through the town center. Most villagers lived in primitive, cramped houses constructed from stone and dried mud. Erected in 1538 by Spanish missionaries, the most impressive building in town was the Catholic church, Parroquia del Divino Salvador. One of Carlos' earliest memories is of riding on the back of his father's bicycle to the ancient house of worship to watch José perform in the church orchestra.

In the Autlán de Navarro of Carlos' youth, most townsmen struggled to eke out a living for themselves and their families by cultivating maize (corn), wheat, or other food crops or by raising livestock. José Santana, however, had found another way to support his growing brood, which would eventually number seven—four girls and three boys. To the immense pride of his young son Carlos, José was a professional musician.

JOSÉ SANTANA, PROFESSIONAL MUSICIAN

José Santana came from a long line of musicians. His great-grandfather, grandfather, and father had all played music professionally at one time or another during their lives. José was born in 1913 in Cuautla in the central Mexican state of Morelos. His father, Antonino, who played the French horn in the local municipal band, taught the boy to read music and play the violin at a young age. José proved a quick study. After the family moved to Autlán de Navarro, José was awarded a

Mariachi bands such as this one often perform for audiences in the city streets of Mexico. Mariachi music originated in Carlos Santana's home state of Jalisco and the upbeat songs often recount everyday pleasures and hardships of life in the Mexican countryside.

place in the local symphony orchestra when he was still a teenager. Soon the young man began hiring himself out to play at weddings, baptisms, patriotic celebrations, and other private and civic functions in his hometown and nearby communities. By the time he married Josefina Barragán in 1940, 27-year-old José was a respected and sought-after musician in the Autlán area.

The music played by José and his various ensembles was a highly danceable mestizaje, or blend of Native American traditions and European cultural influences. German polkas and waltzes and Spanish tangos figured prominently in the ensembles' repertoires; so, too, did the famous Mexican folk music that had its roots in Carlos Santana's home state of Jalisco—the mariachi.

Mariachi music is believed to have developed near the city of Guadalajara sometime during the early nineteenth century. The earliest mariachi ensembles used a variety of stringed instruments, including native folk harps and two European imports—violins and guitars—to produce lively, upbeat songs and dances with a strong rhythm and distinctly New World flavor. Eventually, trumpets would also become part of the ensembles. Mariachi songs, based on the Afro-Cuban song form, the son, told of love, death, politics, and the everyday pleasures and hardships of life in the Mexican countryside. By the late 1920s, when José launched his musical career, mariachi bands were more popular than ever, having attracted a loyal following in Mexico's chief cities, as well as its rural areas. The bands, which ranged in size from 5 to 15 musicians, typically dressed in the traditional costume of the Mexican horseman or *charro*—ankle-high boots, tight slacks, elaborately embroidered short jackets, and wide-brimmed sombreros.

By the time Carlos was born, José had added another type of music to his already extensive repertoire: swing. A smooth and danceable style of jazz, swing was wildly popular in the United States from the mid-1930s through the mid-1940s and soon became all the rage south of the border as well. José helped form a new band, Los Cardinales, to play the trendy swing music, along with the more traditional polkas, waltzes, and mariachi pieces that had long been his stock-in-trade. Los Cardinales traveled to cities and resort towns throughout central and northern Mexico, performing at restaurants, civic events, and private gatherings. Often the group would play for tips in the central plazas of the towns they passed through. Joining Los Cardinales meant a bigger and more reliable income for José. But to the dismay of his family, and especially of his adoring middle son Carlos, José's involvement with the new band also meant that he was often away from home for days and even weeks at a time.

Carlos and His Father

Without question, José Santana was young Carlos' greatest hero. "It is true," he reflected recently. "Your dad becomes your first God."[5] Talented and charming, José was "the darling of the town," Carlos recalled. "My memories of [Autlán de Navarro] were that everybody just loved my dad."[6] José was something of a local celebrity and everybody wanted him to play for their weddings, baptisms, or anniversaries. Even the poorest families in Autlán de Navarro would scrimp and save in order to hire José Santana for a special event.

Carlos, who often accompanied his father to his gigs in Autlán and nearby towns, was in awe of the emotional, almost spiritual, impact that José's playing seemed to have on others. Traditional Mexican culture has always placed a high value on music. For the country's downtrodden masses, music is viewed not only as an accompaniment to life's great moments but as vital to a person's sense of well-being. Live music—and the dancing that usually goes with it in Mexico—brightens the drudgery of daily existence and allows men and women to forget their troubles, at least for a while. Even as a young child, Carlos sensed the extraordinary influence that his father and his music had on his impoverished neighbors in Autlán de Navarro. José realized he had the ability to lift his listeners out of their frustration and despair. "I remember watching how people's eyes would light up when my father played the violin," he says of his early years in Autlán. "At that point, I knew he had the power to validate people's existence."[7]

When Carlos was five years old, José began teaching him how to read music and play the violin, just as his own father had done for him when he was a boy. Soon Carlos was playing the violin alongside his father in the church orchestra. Carlos' obvious appreciation and aptitude for music served to strengthen the bond between father and son. "I felt I was the apple of his eye. I felt like I could get away with more. I don't know if it's because I was lighter in skin, like my mom, or because he knew I was going to be a musician. He was less tolerant of everyone else, but he would give me just a little more clutch not to grind the gears,"[8] Carlos revealed to *Rolling Stone* magazine. "Somehow, there was always a connection between him and me," Santana recalled, "he loved the whole family, but there's always one who's more endearing and I guess I was it."[9]

José Goes North

In 1954, José Santana's never-ending search for work took him to the bustling border town of Tijuana in the northwestern state of Baja California Norte. Just 18 miles from San Diego, Tijuana had been a popular destination for Americans—and especially Californians—ever since gambling was legalized in the city during the early twentieth century. After the Eighteenth Amendment to the Constitution was passed in 1919 prohibiting the manufacture, sale, and consumption of alcoholic beverages in the United States, tourism boomed in Tijuana as thirsty Americans streamed across the border to the city's numerous bars and nightclubs. Even after the U.S. Congress repealed the Eighteenth Amendment in 1933 and Mexico's reforming president Lázaro Cárdenas shut down the city's casinos five years later, Tijuana remained a magnet for American *turistas*. Eager for a taste of Mexican culture, visitors from nearby San Diego and Los Angeles flocked to Tijuana to dine at one of the city's numerous restaurants or shop at its souvenir stores and colorful outdoor markets. Many Americans were also drawn to the border town's seamy nightlife. By the 1950s, Tijuana's longtime reputation as a playground for "sinful" tourism had grown stronger than ever as brothels and strip joints multiplied along its main drag, the

Avenida Revolución, and the city developed a thriving illegal drug trade.

When José told her that he intended to look for work in Tijuana, Josefina had been enthusiastic. She hoped that if José did well in Tijuana, he would move the entire family there. Josefina's desire to relocate the family to Tijuana was based on a fundamental misunderstanding. Having little knowledge of the world beyond her hometown, Josefina believed that Tijuana was located on the northern side of the border, in the United States, a fabled land where freedom and economic opportunity were said to abound.

As weeks stretched into months and José had still not sent for her and the children, however, Josefina began to feel uneasy. It was evident that her husband had found steady employment in Tijuana because he was sending money to her on a regular basis. Nevertheless, in the brief notes that accompanied the money, José said nothing about when he might return to Autlán de Navarro. Nor did he discuss the possibility of moving the entire family north anytime soon. José's ever-lengthening absence was particularly hard on six-year-old Carlos, who missed his father terribly. Carlos would imagine José hugging him. Sometimes, in hopes of feeling closer to his distant father, he would walk around the house holding a belt or other article of clothing on which the faint scent of José's cologne still lingered.

Josefina Takes Matters into Her Own Hands

By the summer of 1955, José had been gone for nearly a year. Josefina decided the time had come to take matters into her own hands. She hauled all of the family's furniture onto the street and sold every piece of it. Then she took her meager earnings to the owner of a small cab business in town. "José told me to give you this money and said for you to bring us to Tijuana, and when you see him he'll give you the rest of the money," Josefina informed the man. "Of course, it was a lie," Carlos later told *Billboard* magazine, and the owner of the cab business was immediately suspicious. "That's funny," the man said to Josefina, "because I got a letter from José the other day, and he didn't say anything to me about this." Josefina was unfazed. Pulling an envelope out of her skirt pocket, she replied, "Well, he said so in this letter here that he sent to ME." When the owner demanded that she hand over the envelope so that he could see for himself what José had written, Josefina hotly refused, declaring that the letter from her husband was "private."[10]

Somehow, Josefina finally managed to convince the reluctant cab driver to take her and her seven young children on the 1,000-mile trip from Autlán to Tijuana. After spending two miserable days on the road crammed into the cab driver's beat-up station wagon, the Santanas at last reached the outskirts of Tijuana. A short time later, the excited group arrived at the address that Josefina had copied from the envelope of José's last letter home. But when Josefina knocked on the door of the house where her husband was supposed to be living and asked for José Santana, the family was in for a bitter surprise. The woman who answered the door said that she did not know anyone by that name; Josefina must have the wrong place, she insisted. "My mom broke down," Carlos recalled decades later. "'What are we gonna do?'" she sobbed. "'We don't have any money to go back.'"[11]

Just when all seemed lost, a passerby took pity on the distraught woman and asked her if he could help. When Carlos' mother showed him a photograph of José, the man immediately recognized him and assured Josefina that she had the right place after all. "You look like a nice family," the man said kindly. "Knock again. He'll come out." This time when Josefina rapped on the door, however, the woman stormed out of the house screaming, "What do you want? I told you he's not here!" Suddenly Carlos spotted his bleary-eyed father at an upstairs window, looking as though he had just woken from a long nap. When José caught sight of his wife and seven children in the street below, remembered Carlos, "I saw my dad's face become like the NBC peacock rainbow, turning all the different colors of surprise, joy, frustration, anger, fear—everything."[12] The family had been reunited at last, but to eight-year-old Carlos, their future together appeared frighteningly uncertain.

A Difficult Time for the Santanas

For the next several weeks, José and Josefina barely spoke to one another. Josefina was deeply wounded by her husband's faithlessness. On his part, José was furious with his wife for bringing the family to Tijuana without first obtaining his permission. In the machismo social order of mid-twentieth-century Mexico, the father was the undisputed ruler of the family. A man's ability to completely dominate his spouse and children was considered as essential proof of his manliness. Moreover, in traditional Mexican society, it was common for married men to take mistresses, and a good wife was expected to quietly endure her husband's infidelity.

While José stubbornly went on living with his mysterious woman friend, Josefina and the children rented a house that was under construction in Colonia Libertad, one of Tijuana's most notorious slums. The house had no windows and the roof was only half finished. To make matters worse, Josefina and the children were forced to sleep on the floor because there was not a single piece of furniture in the place. Once or twice a week, José would stop by to drop off groceries. From the beginning, he made it clear that he expected Carlos and his older brother Tony to help meet the family's expenses now that they were in Tijuana. "He bought a bunch of Chiclets gum," Carlos recalled, "broke it in half, and gave one half to me and one to my older brother, saying, 'Don't come back until you've sold them all.' I thought, oh, so that's my reality now . . ."[13]

Gradually, José's visits to his family became more frequent until he was coming by nearly every day. "I have a feeling that I was a big part of that because I was my dad's darling," Carlos later mused: "I kept looking at him during his brief visits and he kept looking at me."[14] Finally, three or four months after the children and their mother had arrived in the border city, José and Josefina reconciled. Soon after, the Santanas moved into a better house in downtown Tijuana.

After the move to the new neighborhood, Carlos began attending a local Catholic elementary school. The nuns and priests who taught there were harsh disciplinarians and eight-year-old Carlos came to dread school. Taking the traditional adage, "spare the rod, spoil the child" as their motto, they relied heavily on corporal punishment to keep their pupils in line. Children were routinely slapped or rapped on the knuckles with wooden rulers for such minor infractions as talking out of turn. Carlos complained to his parents about the severe treatment he and his classmates received from their teachers, but José and Josefina were unsympathetic. During the 1950s, most Catholic educators considered physical punishment an essential ingredient of forming good character among their young charges. Corporal discipline was part of school, Carlos' parents told their son, and he would have to learn to live with it.

After his school day was finished, Carlos attended classes at a local music college. Paying for them placed a strain on the family's already tight budget, but José was determined to do all he could to encourage his middle son's obvious aptitude for music. At first, Carlos' instructors pushed him to learn the clarinet. Carlos, however, took an instant dislike to the instrument. Finally, the boy's teachers and father agreed that Carlos should focus on the violin instead.

José spent many hours with Carlos each week tutoring him in the violin. At the music college, Carlos focused on the works of classical European composers such as Ludwig van Beethoven and Wolfgang Amadeus Mozart. At home, José also drilled his son in the traditional music of Mexico, and particularly the popular mariachi songs for which Carlos' home state of Jalisco was famous.

Tijuana's Avenida Revolución is a popular tourist destination for those who make the trip to Latin America's most northern town. During his youth, Carlos and two other boys charged 50 cents a song to play for the American visitors who frequented the border town's main drag.

To his father's delight, Carlos made rapid progress with his music lessons. By the boy's tenth birthday, José believed that Carlos was ready to play the violin professionally. After school and on weekends, Carlos joined his father on Tijuana's main drag, the Avenida Revolución, where they played traditional Mexican songs for the American tourists. After a while, José began sending his son out on his own to entertain the turistas. Carlos soon joined forces with two other boys, both guitarists. The young trio charged 50 cents a song and obligingly performed whatever their audience wanted to hear. They often ended up by playing the same songs over and over again. Carlos was understandably bored and restless with this routine. Nonetheless, he knew that his family needed the money he earned as a street musician and was determined not to let them down.

Carlos Rebels

As Carlos' repertoire of popular Mexican songs and dances grew, José decided to take the boy along with him to the cantinas (bars), where his band played on weekend evenings. To

CARLOS SANTANA'S ADVICE TO YOUNG MUSICIANS AND SONGWRITERS

In an interview conducted by author Bill Demain in 2003 for his book, *In Their Own Words: Songwriters Talk about the Creative Process*, Carlos Santana gave the following advice to aspiring musicians and songwriters:

[Y]ou've got to get your connections together. You've got to get out of the bed, out of the chair, and learn where the switches are in the house, so you can turn on the lights and see what you're doing. By that metaphor, I mean, learn to implement, activate, ignite, and infuse spiritual principles in your everyday life. You say, "What . . . does that mean?" It means for you to get off your butt and don't let somebody else do it for you. It means to make the effort to correct your thought patterns . . . and connect.

. . . Why are you playing music? You want to be rich and famous? That's lame. . . . But if you really, really want to make a difference in the world and do something where you have respect everywhere you go and you feel good about yourself in the morning and the evening before you go to bed, then work with your music, for the right reasons. It's not how fast you play, or how slick, or how hip. Use music to complement life, to raise people's consciousness. That's the most important thing that you can do.*

* Bill Demain, *In Their Own Words: Songwriters Talk about the Creative Process* (Westport, Conn.: Praeger, 2004), 78.

Carlos' dismay, the saloons where his father worked always seemed to be in the seediest part of town. Four decades later, Santana still had vivid memories of the squalid cantinas: "No floor, just dirt. Tables black from cigarettes because they didn't have . . . ashtrays. And a cop with his hat backward like rappers do, putting his hand on the prostitutes' private parts right in front of me . . . and she can't do anything because otherwise he'll arrest her. My stomach just got really, really sick at the smell, the whole thing."[15]

Carlos was also disgusted by the drunken customers' disrespectful attitude toward his father. They talked and laughed loudly during his sets and invariably some drunk would offer José money to play his favorite song six or seven times in a row. Carlos knew that his family needed the extra cash, yet he still felt humiliated for his father when José accepted the money. "When I grow up," Carlos promised himself, "I'm going to play what I want to play and they're still going to pay me or I'll be doing something else."[16]

José and his band mostly played mariachi songs at the cantinas because that was what the audience, and especially the American customers, wanted to hear. As time went on, Carlos became increasingly frustrated with the mariachi pieces. There is little opportunity "for free expression or improvisation in mariachi playing," notes writer Simon Leng, "the violinist is meant to stick to the melody, play a few standard lead-in notes for the singer and that is about it."[17] To Carlos' profound irritation, whenever he tried to add an improvised flourish of his own or strayed even a little from the main melody, his father would sternly silence him.

One night Carlos finally decided that he had had enough. "I don't wanna be here," he told his father. "I don't want to live this kind of scene. Look at where we are, just smell it! Do you think that this scene is better than anything else?"[18] That was the first time Carlos had dared to speak back to his parent, and he was sure that his father was going to slap him. Instead, José quietly told his son to go home; he would not try to force Carlos to play in the cantinas any longer. "It was as if I had opened his eyes,"[19] Carlos would reflect years later. Carlos Santana had taken the first step in declaring his independence from his father and his father's music. He was ready to start looking for his own musical path.

3

Finding a Musical Path

To help support the family, Carlos continued to play violin for the turistas on Avenida Revolución after quitting his father's band. He was rapidly losing his taste for the mariachi songs that were the stock-in-trade of a Tijuana street musician, however. "For some reason, the traditional Mexican music just wouldn't go inside my body; it would not accept it," he recalled. "It was like somebody else's shoes or somebody else's teeth. I just didn't want to touch it."[20]

DISCOVERING THE BLUES

By the time he was 11 years old, Carlos had fallen in love with a new kind of music from the United States: the blues. First made popular in the early 1900s by southern Afro-Americans, such as W.C. Handy and Jelly Roll Morton, the blues evolved from slave work songs and spirituals. Based on a distinctive scale that blends minor and major chords, the blues typically feature a slow, melancholy melody, lyrics that forcefully convey both suffering and defiance, and a syncopated rhythm. (In syncopation, accents—emphases on particular notes or chords—are placed on weak beats and at various, unexpected points in the measure.)

Carlos first discovered blues music from listening to the radio stations of nearby San Diego. He soon became a devoted fan of popular blues and rhythm-and-blues artists such as Muddy Waters, T-Bone Walker, John Lee Hooker, Bobby "Blue" Bland, and above all, B.B. King. (Rhythm and blues—or R&B—is a style of black music that combines elements of jazz and blues and is generally performed with electronically amplified instruments.)

Widely considered one of the greatest blues guitarists of all time, B.B. King was born in rural Mississippi in 1925. By the late 1950s, he had a string of R&B hits and was a regular on the "chitlin circuit," a group of black nightclubs that stretched across the American South and Midwest. Carlos was particularly captivated by King's almost eerie ability to imitate the human voice with his electric guitar. "B.B. King . . . knocked me right out," Carlos later remembered of his first introduction to the bluesman on the radio in Tijuana. "As soon as I heard a guitar player like that, I thought 'Man, that's the stuff—this is the sort of music I want to do when I grow up.'"[21]

JOSÉ HEADS NORTH AGAIN

Convinced that a better life awaited her family on the other side of the Mexican-American border, Josefina had never relinquished her dream of immigrating to the United States. In 1961, she came one step closer to realizing her dream when José traveled to San Francisco in search of work.

Over the past three decades, immigrants from Mexico and all over Latin America had been flooding into the San Francisco Bay Area. By the early 1960s, a large and vibrant Hispanic community had developed in the city's Mission District neighborhood and that was where José headed in 1961. The Santanas agreed that once José had established himself as a musician in the Mission District, Josefina and the children would follow him to San Francisco.

As far as 13-year-old Carlos was concerned, the one good thing about his father going to the United States was that he would no longer have to practice the violin every day. The rebellious teenager had developed as strong an aversion to his father's instrument of choice as he had to the traditional Mexican music that was José's specialty. Indeed, it had gotten to the point where Carlos could hardly even stand the smell or the feel of the violin.

A BRIEF HISTORY OF THE BLUES

Blues music, which derives from traditional Afro-American spiritual and work songs, first gained widespread popularity in the United States during the early twentieth century. Blues got its name from the extensive use of half-flatted or blues notes, which gives the music an effect of fluctuating between the minor and major modes.

Early blues artists included Jelly Roll Morton and W.C. Handy, whose compositions "Memphis Blues" and "St. Louis Blues" became major hits in the United States just before World War I. The very first blues recording, "Crazy Blues," performed by Mamie Smith, was released in 1920. During the 1920s, Smith and other blues singers developed what came to be known as "classic" blues. Rooted in urban America, classic blues were typically composed by professional songwriters and sung by female vaudeville performers. The second major blues tradition that developed during the 1920s was "country" blues, which included the highly emotional Mississippi Delta Blues and the more rhythmic and precise style of playing, dubbed the Texas Blues. The most famous Texan Blues performer of the post-World War I era was Lightnin' Hopkins, one of Carlos Santana's earliest musical heroes.

CARLOS TAKES UP THE ELECTRIC GUITAR

Soon after José left for San Francisco, Josefina took Carlos to a free concert at the plaza near the Palacio Municipal, Tijuana's old city hall. Someone had told her that the T.J.'s, a local band that specialized in the R&B music Carlos was always listening to on the radio, would be playing.

Carlos was captivated by the energetic young band: "The sound of the electric guitars, amps and everything . . . for me it was like watching a flying saucer for the first time."[22] Carlos was particularly enthralled by the group's 16-year-old lead guitarist,

During the Great Depression of the 1930s, thousands of blacks moved from the rural South to Chicago and other northern cities in search of work. In time, many blues musicians who had migrated north, and particularly those who settled in Chicago, developed a new style of "urban" blues featuring a louder, denser sound and lyrics that centered on the trials and tribulations of Afro-American urban life.

After World War II, many urban blues musicians, including Carlos Santana's great musical idols B.B. King and Muddy Waters, switched from the acoustic guitar to the electric guitar. By about 1950, some urban blues performers had added a strong dance beat to their music, creating an immensely popular new style of blues called rhythm and blues (R&B). Leading R&B artists of the 1950s included Ray Charles, Chuck Berry, Little Richard, and B.B. King. During the same decade, Elvis Presley, Jerry Lee Lewis, and other white performers developed R&B into rock and roll. By the mid-1960s, Afro-American performers like Otis Redding and Marvin Gaye had taken R&B in a different direction, turning it into soul and funk.

During the early 1960s, Javier Batiz, pictured here in a 2000 photo, played lead guitar for the T.J.'s, a Tijuana band that specialized in rhythm and blues (R&B). When Carlos was in his early teens, he attended all the band's free concerts at the plaza near Tijuana's city hall and was captivated by Batiz's skillful technique on the electric guitar.

Javier Batiz, who sported a leather jacket, tight "drainpipe" jeans, and a high pompadour hairdo copied from the flamboyant R&B artist Little Richard. To Carlos' delight, Batiz and his band covered the songs of America's most popular rhythm-and-blues performers, including Chuck Berry, Ray Charles, and B.B. King.

Carlos was so impressed by Batiz's technique on the electric guitar that he soon became the teenage musician's most loyal fan, attending all of his band's free concerts at the plaza, as well as its regular weekend gigs at the Latino-American Club in downtown Tijuana. "Carlos's got the music bug again!"[23] Josefina wrote happily to José in San Francisco. Eager to encourage his son's revived enthusiasm for music, José bought a second-hand electric guitar and mailed the instrument to Carlos. Although the guitar was more than a little beat-up, Carlos was thrilled with his father's present.

Over the next few months, Carlos devoted himself to learning how to play the electric guitar. Because of his extensive training on the violin, he was able to master the new instrument with relative ease. Soon he could pick out many of his favorite tunes from the radio and was emulating the sounds of his blues and R&B idols, B.B. King, T-Bone Walker, John Lee Hooker, and Muddy Waters. Determined to learn as much as he could about the technique of blues guitar, he scrutinized Javier Batiz's performances. Years later, Batiz would claim that he had tutored Carlos in the electric guitar, but Santana remembered differently: Javier "was sort of stingy," he reminisced. "If I was looking where he was playing, he would turn the other way so I could not see the chords he was playing."[24]

EL CONVOY

Carlos progressed rapidly with the electric guitar and was soon invited to join a local R&B band called the Strangers. "I started out playing electric bass . . . because the leader of the band owned all the equipment and told us who would play what," Carlos recalled. "But after a while people told him that I played too many notes for the bass and he should let me play guitar."[25] The band performed at dances and other small local gigs and often found themselves competing for jobs with the T.J.'s.

After Carlos had been with the Strangers for a few months, he landed a steady job playing with the house band at a strip joint called El Convoy. On weekdays, the 13-year-old headed straight from school to the sleazy club on Avenida Revolución. The band played for an hour and then the strippers performed for an hour.

The musicians and the strippers went back and forth like this until midnight. On weekends, the club stayed open all night and Carlos would not make it home until 6 A.M. or later.

On Sunday mornings, Carlos hurried home from the strip club to change his clothes and grab his violin before heading to Tijuana's Catholic cathedral to play in the church orchestra. "That contrast gave me a nice balance," Santana mused recently. "That's where I learned about dignity."[26] At Sunday Mass he would see the prostitutes who frequented El Convoy proudly escorting their children to the front of the church to take Communion. The boys and girls were always dressed immaculately, often in pristine white. "I've learned from traveling around the world that dignity is something that a lot of royalty, a lot of real queens, don't have as compared to those Tijuana prostitutes when it comes to taking care of their own children," Santana now says. "That's why I don't judge a book by its cover anymore. . . .You can't buy class."[27]

For Carlos, working at El Convoy had its drawbacks. The hours were grueling and the audience was typically drunk and rowdy. In Tijuana, the kind of rough-and-tumble men who frequented the Convoy were known as the "cut and shoot crowd": If they didn't like you, they would not hesitate to knife you or shoot you. Yet, if the Convoy's clientele left much to be desired, the pay was good. Carlos' weekly paycheck of nine dollars was significantly more than he had made when he was a street musician and went a long way toward meeting the family's expenses.

Even more important to Carlos than the money he earned at El Convoy was the musical education he was acquiring at the strip joint. "There were a lot of black American musicians who'd go to Tijuana . . . to score some drugs," Santana recalled. "They'd spend all their money and then not want to come back to the U.S. until they'd made a little money, so they'd stay and play in the club."[28] Some of the Americans were accomplished blues or R&B guitarists, and Carlos absorbed invaluable lessons in expression, timing, and rhythm from watching them perform. Carlos was also able to pick up the latest hits by his favorite U.S. artists from the visiting musicians, including B.B. King's "Sweet Sixteen" and Ray Charles' "Georgia on My Mind." "I got a big education at . . . the Convoy," Santana says today: "It was tough but I ended up learning a lot."[29]

SAN FRANCISCO

In 1962, Josefina and José decided the time had come to move the entire family north. Josefina obtained immigration papers for herself and the children, and informed Carlos that they would be moving to San Francisco that summer.

Carlos was dismayed. He had no desire to leave his native country and he especially did not want to leave his job at El Convoy. Carlos begged to be allowed to stay behind in Tijuana. He could easily support himself on his earnings from El Convoy, he argued. Josefina, however, insisted that he emigrate with the rest of the family. Carlos would have greater educational and economic opportunities on the other side of the border, she said, and anyway, he was too young to live on his own.

Carlos hardly spoke to his mother during the long drive to San Francisco. After the family moved into their new Mission District apartment and he discovered that Josefina had spent the $300 he had saved for a new electric guitar on the first month's rent, Carlos was even angrier. To make matters worse, when the new school year started in September, 15-year-old Carlos was placed back in junior high instead of being allowed to attend senior high with his peers. Carlos' English skills were not strong enough for high school, the superintendent said.

Not surprisingly, Carlos was miserable at his new school: "It was a drag. . . . I had to adapt to a whole other way of thinking and being around kids, because I thought I was a man of the world after playing in a nightclub in Tijuana. . . . To me, I was a grown-up, but when I came here, I had to live the life of a young adolescent all over again, and I couldn't relate."[30] Finally, after three months of nonstop complaining from Carlos, Josefina had had enough. She handed Carlos a $20 bill and told him he could go back to Tijuana.

THE VIRGIN OF GUADALUPE

After spending most of the day on the road, Carlos arrived in downtown Tijuana shortly after sundown on October 31, 1962. As he stepped off the bus, an eerie scene confronted him. The dark streets of the city teemed with ghosts, skeletons, and were-wolves: revelers off to celebrate the first night of Mexico's three-day-long festival, Los Dias de los Muertos (The Days of the Dead), in the seedy bars and nightclubs of Avenida Revolución.

All of a sudden, Carlos felt scared and very vulnerable: "It dawned on 15-year-old me: 'I'm alone. . . . I don't know any-body here as far as family.'"[31] Instinctively, he headed for Tijuana's central Catholic shrine, La Catedral Nuestra Señora de Guadalupe. If anyone could help him now, he thought, it was the dark-skinned Virgin Mother in whose honor the cathedral was named.

The legend of the Virgin of Guadalupe goes back to 1531, a decade after Hernán Cortés and his army conquered the Aztec Empire. According to the story, one day an Indian peas-ant named Juan Diego was walking through a desolate area northwest of Mexico City. Suddenly, on the crest of a small hill, Diego saw a vision of a radiant woman with Indian features and a brown complexion. The woman spoke to Diego in his native language of Náhuatl, identifying herself as Mary, the Mother of the True God, Jesus Christ. She instructed the peas-ant to go to the Bishop's Palace in Mexico City and tell the prelate to build a temple in her honor on the hill. At first, the bishop refused to accept the word of a humble Indian. But when an image of the Virgin miraculously appeared on the white fabric of Diego's tilma or cloak, the Spanish prelate was convinced. During the first ten years of Spanish rule in Mexico, relatively few Indians converted to their conquerors' Catholic faith. After hearing the story of the dark-skinned, Náhuatl-speaking Virgin, however, hundreds of thousands of Native Mexicans embraced Christianity, and churches bearing the Virgin's name were erected thoughout the country.

Carlos' Prayer Is Answered

Over the centuries, the Virgin of Guadalupe, as the dark-skinned Madonna came to be known, would become the patron saint of the Mexican people. Not only did she offer hope and a sense of dignity to the nation's poor and down-trodden masses, but it was said that prayers to the Virgin were more powerful than virtually any other expression of faith. It was natural, then, that the young Carlos should turn to Our Lady of Guadalupe in his time of need.

On entering the cathedral, Carlos immediately made his way to the front of the church, where a large statue of the Virgin stood. "Virgin Mother, I was here a year ago with my brother," he prayed. "We walked on our knees from the front door all the way to your altar. I didn't ask for a favor then, so I figure you owe me one. So I ask that you give me my job back while I'm here, and take care of my family in California."[32]

After lingering in the cathedral a little longer, Carlos gathered his courage and set out for El Convoy. When he reached his old place of employment, the club manager was not encouraging. He knew that Josefina had recently moved to the United States and that Carlos was underage. If he hired Carlos, Josefina might send the police after him, the manager said. But when Carlos produced a letter of permission from his mother, the manager relented. "Hey!" he yelled to a glum-faced fellow who was strumming a guitar onstage. "You can go home, man, Carlos is gonna take over!"[33]

CARLOS ON HIS OWN

Now that he had his old job back, Carlos had to find a place to live. At first, he shared a room in a rundown hotel with the drummer from El Convoy's band. Within a few months, however, the two had been kicked out—presumably for playing their music too loud. Fortunately for Carlos, one of his mother's friends from the old neighborhood took pity on the boy and invited him to live with her family.

During the day, Carlos slept or hung out at the beach. Like

other teenagers of his era, he loved to browse through hot rod journals and the humor magazine *Mad*. On Sunday afternoons, he attended the bullfights at El Toreo de Tijuana. Seven nights a week, he could be found at El Convoy, playing the guitar with the house band and any visiting musician who needed to earn a few dollars before heading back home to San Diego or Los Angeles. "I was really learning again," Santana recently recalled of his second stint at El Convoy: "The house band was learning things like "Call It Stormy Monday" [by T-Bone Walker] and "You Can Make It if You Try" [by Gene Allison]. I was picking up all kinds of musical repertoire. I was really confident about what I knew about music."[34]

SAN FRANCISCO AGAIN

When Carlos had been in Tijuana for a year, his parents decided it was time for their middle son to rejoin the family. In the autumn of 1963, shortly before President John F. Kennedy was assassinated, Josefina and Carlos' older brother Tony drove down to Tijuana to bring the 16-year-old home. Carlos was dismayed when they tracked him down at El Convoy. He did not want to go, he told his mother. He liked his job and was getting along very well on his own, he insisted.

But Josefina had made up her mind—her son was coming home. She ordered Tony, who was considerably larger than Carlos, to get his brother into the car, one way or another. "They actually kidnapped me," Carlos recalled years later. "My brother grabbed me—my legs were dangling—[and] put me in the car."[35]

For two months, Carlos hardly spoke to his parents. In exasperation, Josefina finally gave him $20 for bus fare and told him to go back to Mexico. This time around, however, Carlos had second thoughts. "I got as far as Mission Street," Santana remembered, "and my stomach said, 'You don't want to go back over there to Tijuana, man.'"[36] Carlos had decided to give life in the United States a chance at last.

A NEW SCHOOL AND A NEW GUITAR

Adjusting to his new life in San Francisco was not easy for Carlos. By early 1964, his English had improved to the point that he was able to enroll in senior high school. Yet, although Carlos was relieved to be attending school with boys and girls his own age, he still struggled to relate to his classmates at Mission High. After spending a year working and living on his own in the adult world, Carlos felt too old for his peers. The things they talked about—playing hooky or hot-wiring cars—seemed childish and silly. Worst of all, few of Carlos' fellow students appeared to have any interest in music beyond the current top-40 radio hits, and especially the surfer songs of the popular California group the Beach Boys. To Carlos' disgust, he quickly discovered that most of his classmates had never even heard of B.B. King or Bobby Bland, although they had the lyrics to "Surfin' Safari" and "Surfin' U.S.A." down cold. "I was extremely frustrated when I came [to San Francisco] because the main music that was happening was the Beach Boys, surfing music, and I hated it,"[37] Santana remembered.

Carlos' mood only worsened when one of Tony's friends accidentally sat on his Gibson Les Paul guitar and broke it in half. Carlos had used some of his hard-won earnings from El Convoy to purchase the guitar in Tijuana less than a year earlier, and the instrument was his pride and joy. Carlos was still simmering a few nights later when Tony, who had to report to work early the next morning, came in late from a party and wanted to go to bed immediately. Carlos and his brothers and sisters were engrossed in a horror flick when Tony stormed into the living room of the family's tiny apartment and switched off the television set, just minutes before the movie was to have ended. A scuffle erupted and Carlos gave Tony a black eye.

That night, Carlos lay awake waiting for retaliation from his big brother, who was also his bedmate. But Tony did nothing; indeed, he was unnaturally quiet. Carlos was still feeling nervous when he arrived home from school the next day to find his brother waiting for him in the living room. To Carlos'

Rhythm-and-blues guitarist/songwriter B.B. King, who is pictured here in a 1990 photo, was a big influence on Carlos during his formative years. Carlos was captivated by King's ability to imitate the human voice with his electric guitar and hoped to one day play just like his hero.

amazement, Tony handed him a big package. When he opened it, Carlos discovered a brand-new Gibson Les Paul electric guitar. "I broke down," Santana remembered. Tony, embarrassed by this uncharacteristic display of emotion from his younger brother, merely said, "You're gonna pay for it—I just paid the down payment."[38]

THE BATTLE OF THE BANDS

By the end of 1964, Carlos had formed a new band with two other young men from the Mission District: Dan Haro, a drummer, and Gus Rodrigues, a bass guitarist. Haro, who came from a well-off family, had originally recruited Carlos for the band by promising to buy him a new amplifier if Santana would teach him and Rodrigues everything he knew about the blues and R&B. Soon the combo was performing at small parties and weddings in the Bay Area.

In 1965, Santana, Haro, and Rodrigues decided to link up with a local singer named Joyce Dunn. Dunn, who would eventually join the popular band, Sly and the Family Stone, specialized in covering the latest soul hits. Soul is a style of vocal music that first became popular in the mid-1960s. Rooted in R&B and gospel music, it is characterized by searing vocal power and lyrics that relate the day-to-day experiences and problems of black Americans in down-to-earth language.

Shortly after Dunn joined the group, Santana, Haro, and Rodrigues heard about a "battle of the bands" contest being sponsored by a local radio station. Although several hundred bands entered the contest, Santana's group managed to make it to the top three. The final round of the contest was held at the Cow Palace, one of the city's largest concert venues. Seventeen-year-old Carlos and his fellow band members were thrilled by their success. But as the group waited their turn to play, "the worst thing happened," Santana recalled: "We got excited, we got nervous, so we got drunk."[39] The band missed a number of chord changes and was promptly eliminated. Just the fact that the group had gotten as far as it had filled Carlos with confidence, however. He was beginning to believe that he really had a future as a musician after all.

4

A San Francisco Sensation

Shortly after the battle of the bands contest, Carlos Santana met a young man from the Mission District who was destined to have a dramatic impact on his career. His name was Stan Marcum, and although not a musician himself, Stan was deeply interested in a wide range of musical styles, including jazz, soul, blues, and rock. Marcum was particularly drawn to the musical and cultural revolution then developing in the neighboring district of Haight-Ashbury, the nerve center of the hippie movement and of what was coming to be known as the "San Francisco Sound." When Stan first took Carlos to the Haight in 1965, the 18-year-old guitarist was immediately enthralled by the district's unique cultural and musical scene: "I found myself wanting to be a part of this new wave,"[40] Santana later recalled. During the course of the next several years, Carlos Santana would not just become a part of San Francisco's new musical wave. He would become one of its brightest stars.

THE SAN FRANCISCO SOUND

Stimulated by a flourishing club scene, a big university population, and the new cultural influences emanating from the
Haight-Ashbury District, San Francisco became a breeding
ground for new rock bands during the 1960s. The so-called
San Francisco Sound emerged during the middle of the
decade, when several groups with ties to the Haight's hippie
community achieved national prominence. Among the best
known of these bands were the Grateful Dead, the Jefferson
Airplane, and Big Brother and the Holding Company, which
featured the legendary blues-rock singer Janis Joplin.

Although each of the leading San Francisco bands had its
own approach to music, they shared a particular consciousness
that was deeply rooted in Haight-Ashbury's hippie lifestyle.
Experimentation with drugs, and especially hallucinogens or
psychedelics such as LSD (popularly known as acid), mescaline, and psilocybin, was central to that shared consciousness,
and the San Francisco Sound both reflected and helped to
spread the Haight's drug culture. Indeed, the music played by
the Grateful Dead and other popular Bay Area bands soon
came to be known as "psychedelic" or "acid rock." In acid rock,
notes historian Edward Rielly, "musical performers attempted
to parallel the effects of LSD . . . by altering normal temporal
dimensions of the songs, changing traditional ensemble patterns to create a less structured performance, increasing vol-
ume, and adding other sensory stimuli such as flashing
lights."[41] Acid rock lyrics were also intended to suggest the psychedelic experience, and some songs even went so far as to
openly promote the use of mind-altering drugs: "feed your
head," the lyrics of the Jefferson Airplane's hit single, "White
Rabbit," boldly suggested.

By 1966, an old concert hall in downtown San Francisco
called the Fillmore Auditorium had become the primary home
of the Jefferson Airplane, the Grateful Dead, Quicksilver
Messenger Service, and the city's other hot new acid rock
bands. Thousands of young people, many of them high on

LSD or marijuana, crammed into the Fillmore every weekend to listen and dance to the hard-driving beat of the San Francisco Sound. Among the most devoted patrons of the wildly popular concert venue were two music-loving teenagers from the Mission District, Stan Marcum and Carlos Santana.

Bill Graham and the Fillmore Auditorium

Carlos' loyalty to the Fillmore was not only rooted in his enthusiasm for the new acid rock sound. What really drew him to the concert venue was the astonishing variety of musical

HALLUCINOGENS IN THE 1960s

During the early 1960s, drug use, which had previously been almost entirely confined to residents of impoverished urban neighborhoods and members of the artistic community, began to gain acceptance among a larger segment of the American population and especially among the nation's youth. The most common drugs used by young people during the decade were hallucinogens, including mescaline from the peyote cactus, psilocybin, which is derived from certain mushrooms, and LSD (acid).

The most potent and popular of the hallucinogens during the 1960s was LSD. LSD was first developed in the late 1930s by a Swiss chemist, who soon discovered that the colorless, odorless, and tasteless chemical could dramatically affect a person's emotions, thinking, and perceptions. The drug was largely forgotten until the early 1960s, however, when Harvard psychology professor Timothy Leary began conducting research on LSD and other psychedelics. Leary became an ardent disciple of LSD, claiming that acid was the path to inner enlightenment and a truer beauty. After losing his teaching position at Harvard, Leary devoted himself to popularizing LSD, which remained legal in the United States until 1966. Tens of thousands of high school styles that he could experience there. At the Fillmore, in addition to the San Francisco Sound bands, Carlos enjoyed performances by blues masters like John Lee Hooker and Jimmy Reed, soul singers like Otis Redding and Aretha Franklin, and distinguished foreign artists like flamenco guitarist Manitas De Plata and sitarist Ravi Shankar. (A type of lute, the sitar is widely used in the classical music of northern India.)

The person responsible for bringing this remarkably diverse slate of performers to the Fillmore was the auditorium's hard-driving manager, Bill Graham. Born in Berlin to

and college students heeded the so-called "Drug Guru's" message to "turn on, tune in, and drop out," and from the mid- to the late 1960s, acid use was common at music concerts and other large gatherings of young people in many parts of the country.

As those who experimented with the drug during the 1960s quickly discovered, LSD's effects are highly unpredictable and depend on the user's mood and personality as well as the amount of the drug ingested. Effects typically last for six to ten hours but can persist considerably longer. Some users suffer from rapid and frightening mood swings, while others report that their sense of time and self are badly distorted by the drug. Sensory perceptions may also become dramatically distorted, causing the user to "see" sounds and "hear" colors. Having an adverse psychological reaction to LSD or other psychedelics (popularly known during the 1960s as a "bad trip") is common. Many users experience overwhelming feelings of helplessness, panic, and confusion. Some researchers now believe that overuse of LSD and other hallucinogens may lead to impaired attention span and memory, depression, and problems with learning and abstract thinking.

Bill Graham, pictured here with Carlos Santana in 1981, managed the Fillmore Auditorium in San Francisco during the 1960s. Graham brought a variety of musicians to the old concert hall, but was most noted for providing a venue for acid-rock groups such as the Grateful Dead, Jefferson Airplane, and Quicksilver Messenger Service.

Russian Jewish parents just two years before Adolph Hitler came to power, Graham's original name was Wolodia Granjonca. Graham's father died as the result of an accident when Bill was just a few days old and his mother perished in a Nazi concentration camp a decade later. During the Nazi Holocaust, 10-year-old Bill trekked on foot all the way from

Marseilles, France, to Lisbon, Portugal, to board a ship to New York City and freedom. Raised by a foster family in a tough, lower-class borough of New York, Graham worked as a cab driver, waiter, and actor before moving to San Francisco in the early 1960s. After producing several highly successful fund-raising concerts for a local acting troupe, Graham decided to devote himself to the music business full time. Savvy and ambitious, he negotiated a long-term lease on the underuti-lized Fillmore Auditorium and recruited the city's up-and-coming rock groups to perform at his new concert-dance hall.

Yet, Graham was more than just a shrewd businessman; he was also a music lover, and his eclectic musical tastes embraced everything from the cutting-edge jazz of Miles Davis to Latin salsa, a spirited dance music with roots in Cuba and Puerto Rico. Determined to educate his youthful audiences about music, Graham made a point of including lesser-known artists on the same bill with the hottest rock acts of the day. Thus, Graham might pair the legendary African-American bluesman Lightnin' Hopkins with the Jefferson Airplane, the brilliant Brazilian gui-tarist Bola Sete with Quicksilver Messenger Service, and sitar virtuoso Ravi Shankar with the Grateful Dead.

Sneaking into the Fillmore

Entranced by the Fillmore's rich musical potpourri, Carlos hated to miss even a single show at Graham's popular venue. Yet paying his way into the theater proved an ongoing chal-lenge for the cash-strapped teen. Soon after moving to San Francisco, Santana took an after-school job as a dishwasher at the Tick-Tock, a local diner. Loyal son that he was, Carlos turned over the bulk of his earnings to his parents. Most weeks, he spent what little remained from his paycheck at the Fillmore box office. When his meager funds were depleted, however, Santana was prepared to go to great lengths to hear his favorite musicians.

Years later, Bill Graham recalled an encounter he had with the young Carlos Santana in his Fillmore office one rainy night in 1966, when the English guitarist Eric Clapton was scheduled to perform:

> There was a marquee . . . and my office was above it. I could open the door and step out and I would be standing on top of the marquee. I heard some noise outside my windows. Somebody was trying the doors. There was a haberdasher [a shop that sells men's clothing] downstairs and a drainpipe you could climb up to get on top of the marquee. . . . I looked out and there were two guys trying to get in. One was Carlos Santana. . . . I'd been asleep at my desk and they woke me up. "Hello?" I said. "Oh jeez," they said. "You know. Like we wanna see the great Eric Clapton, man. But we don't have the bread." They seemed so sincere that I let them in.[42]

Graham's right-hand man at the Fillmore, Paul Baratta, was also won over by Santana and his friend Stan Marcum's obvious devotion to music. Eventually he worked out an arrangement with the two young men so that they would no longer have to sneak into shows that they could not afford to pay for: "At the . . . Jimi Hendrix show . . ., I saw them downstairs four straight nights, plopping down their money. The fifth night they showed up by the ticket booth and I was standing at the top of the stairs. I came down and Stan said, 'Any chance we can get in to see Hendrix? We already paid our way in a few times. We just don't have any more money.'" Baretta could not bring himself to turn Marcum and Santana away. "From that point on," he recalled, "I *always* let them in. They paid when they could and when they couldn't, I let them in anyway."[43]

HIGH SCHOOL

Between washing dishes at the Tick-Tock and hanging out at the Fillmore, Carlos had little time left for homework. School was not a priority for the teenager, as Santana admitted in later years: "Once I got that electric sound, there was no

Another big influence on Santana was Jimi Hendrix, who is pictured here at the Newport Pop Festival in 1969. Carlos once went to the Fillmore five consecutive nights to see the talented electric guitarist, who often played at the San Francisco venue.

turning back. I knew I wasn't going to be an accountant or an English teacher. Even before I came to San Francisco there was nothing that could deter me from this path of music."[44] Many mornings he would leave school as soon as homeroom ended. "They would take attendance and then I'd split,"[45] Santana remembered. On those days when he did stick around, Carlos wiled away most of his time in class daydreaming about playing guitar with B.B. King or Jimi Hendrix.

Not surprisingly, Santana's grades in high school were poor. One class in which he consistently earned top marks, however, was art. Carlos worked diligently in his art classes not only because he enjoyed drawing and painting, but also because he respected his art instructor, Mr. Knudson. The feeling was mutual. "Mr. Knudson believed in me," Santana remembered. "He told me I had a great imagination and a great eye for art."[46] Knudson also told Carlos that he had heard through the grapevine that he was a talented musician.

In 1966, when Carlos was a senior, Knudson gave the teenager some advice he would never forget: "He told me that in the real world, there was no room for fifty-fifty, meaning I had to give 100 percent to become an artist or a musician, to follow my dreams."[47] "When he said that," Santana recalled more than three decades later, "I thought that a person was seeing right through me for the first time. . . . He made me aware that I have this potential. He gave me a quantum leap right there. . . . So I'm really grateful to him."[48]

CARLOS' BIG BREAK

After his conversation with Knudson, Carlos began spending more time than ever at the Fillmore, studying the guitar playing techniques of performers such as Eric Clapton, Jimi Hendrix, and Jerry Garcia of the Grateful Dead. One Sunday afternoon in the spring of 1966, he and Stan Marcum went to the Fillmore to hear another of Carlos' favorite guitarists, Michael Bloomfield of the Butterfield Blues Band. Led by a white harmonica player from Chicago named Paul Butterfield, the Butterfield Blues Band was known for its long, high-volume blues jams.

Santana had been looking forward to the concert for weeks. At the last minute, however, it looked like the performance would have to be canceled when Paul Butterfield showed up at the auditorium high on LSD. As Santana recollected, Butterfield "had no shoes on and looked like he had just seen God and . . . was still watching and beholding Him in the ceiling."[49] With Butterfield obviously in no condition to perform, Graham decided to throw together an impromptu jam session featuring Paul's bandmates and several members of the Jefferson Airplane and the Grateful Dead. When Michael Bloomfield opted to play the keyboards instead of the electric guitar, Stan Marcum had a bold idea. He marched up to Graham and asked him if his guitarist friend from Tijuana could join the group on stage. "He loves playing the blues,"[50] Marcum informed the surprised concert hall manager. Graham brusquely told Marcum that Bloomfield was in charge of the jam session and to ask him.

To Santana's delight Bloomfield agreed to Stan's proposal and even lent Carlos his guitar. "So I got the guitar," Santana remembered, "and stood there, waiting and waiting . . . until they said, 'Oh yeah, you're still here, go ahead and take a solo.' I jumped on it."[51] Bill Graham was immediately captivated by the young guitarist's energy and passion and the distinctive, almost pleading tone he could create by holding a single note for an astonishingly long time, a musical technique Carlos had first acquired as a mariachi violinist in Mexico. After the session ended, Graham asked Carlos if he had a band of his own. Santana replied that he had a drummer and a bass guitarist, which was at least partly true because he still played now and then with Dan Haro and Gus Rodrigues. Graham wrote down Santana's telephone number and told him to bring his band to the Fillmore for a formal audition.

THE SANTANA BLUES BAND

Among the audience that Sunday afternoon was a rhythm guitarist from the suburbs of San Francisco named Tom Frazier. Frazier was trying to put together a band with college student Gregg Rolie, a singer and keyboardist. When Frazier told his friend about the Mexican-American guitarist he had heard at the Fillmore, Gregg urged Tom to track Carlos down. Frazier soon traced Santana to the Tick-Tock and volunteered to drive him to Palo Alto, a wealthy community just south of San

Francisco, to meet Rolie. Santana quickly took Frazier up on his offer; he wanted to put together the best band that he could before auditioning for Graham.

Santana was thrilled to discover that Rolie was almost as familiar with the blues as he was with rock, and the two musicians hit it off at once. Carlos introduced his Mission District compañeros, Haro and Rodrigues, to his new friends from the suburbs and the five young men resolved to form a band. They dubbed themselves the Santana Blues Band, not because they considered Carlos their leader, but because everyone agreed that his last name sounded the best. Soon the group had acquired a sixth member, a Puerto Rican-American street musician and conga player named Michael Carabello.

An integral part of Latin percussion, the conga is a barrel-shaped Cuban drum that is played with the bare hand. The conga's name derives from its African roots: slaves from what is today known as the Democratic Republic of the Congo first brought the drum to the New World four centuries ago. The addition of a conga player to the Santana Blues Band had an immediate and dramatic impact on the group's sound, lending an exotic, Latin flavor to the Santana Blues Band's basic repertoire of blues, R&B, and rock songs.

PLAYING AT THE FILLMORE

Soon the new band was playing gigs at popular San Francisco area dance clubs like the Matrix and the Ark. Audiences were entranced by the group's Latin conga rhythm, which gave the Santana Blues Band a sound unlike any other rock or blues group of the time. By January 1967, Santana and his bandmates believed they were ready to audition for Bill Graham at the Fillmore.

Graham, a longtime fan of Latin music, liked what he heard. He began using the Santana Blues Band as stand-ins whenever one of his scheduled acts canceled. Realizing that the exposure they received at the Fillmore was invaluable, the group jumped at any chance to play at the venue. As Carlos recalled: "Every time somebody would miss [a show], we would be there in a *second*."[52]

Then, just as the band was picking up more and more gigs at the Fillmore, disaster struck. Carlos was diagnosed with tuberculosis, an infectious disease that usually affects the lungs. For two months Carlos languished in the tubercular ward of San Francisco General Hospital while his band gradually fell apart. Haro and Rodrigues, citing family and work obligations, attended fewer and fewer of the group's practices and Carabello stopped showing up for the sessions altogether.

A TIME OF REBUILDING

By the spring of 1967, Carlos felt better and decided he should return to his disintegrating band. His doctors believed otherwise. When they insisted he was not ready to be discharged, Santana took matters into his own hands. He telephoned a friend and asked him to bring him some clothes. After hastily exchanging his hospital gown for jeans and a T-shirt in the elevator, Santana simply strolled out of the building's front entrance.

Soon after Santana made his escape from the hospital, Carlos and Rolie, the two most committed musicians in the Santana Blues Band, decided that some major changes would have to be made in the group's lineup. Haro, Rodrigues, and Carabello were kicked out for failing to attend practices and the band acquired a new drummer and bass guitarist.

A few months later, in June 1967, the Santana Blues Band received its biggest break up to that point when the unit was invited by Bill Graham to open for The Who after the act he had originally scheduled to perform with the superstar band canceled. Carlos and Gregg's moment of triumph was tarnished, however, when the Blues Band's newest members arrived late for the show and Graham hit the roof.

Santana and Rolie quickly concluded that the band was in need of yet another overhaul. Stan Marcum, the group's manager, fired the tardy drummer and bass player, and recruited two new musicians for the band: David Brown, an experienced bass guitarist, and Marcus Malone, a conga drummer from one of San Francisco's meanest slums. Deeply interested in Afro-Cuban music, Malone brought a more authentic Latin flavor to the band's percussion. The band's new lineup was complete when Marcum secured a new rock drummer for the unit, Bob "Doc" Livingston. Soon after, the group decided to drop "Blues Band" from its name and became simply Santana.

MAKING SOME CHANGES IN HIS PERSONAL LIFE

In 1967, in addition to altering his band's lineup, Carlos made some important changes in his personal life. By the summer of that year, Carlos had quit his job at the Tick-Tock and left his parents' home to share a Haight-Ashbury apartment with Stan Marcum and another friend.

Many decades later, Santana would link his decision to move out of his parents' home and give up his day job to two incidents. The first one was hearing his idol B.B. King play blues guitar at the Fillmore. As Santana recalled:

> Seeing B.B. King for the first time at the Fillmore was a revelation. When B.B. King went out there, he got a standing ovation without hitting one note. Everybody stood up and they wouldn't shut up; they just got louder and louder, and I was electrified. . . . When he did hit his first note of the night, it was like a whole other world had opened up. I thought, "Oh, that's how he does it. You go inside yourself to come out with this sound." . . . So I went home and I just said that I had to leave my house.[53]

Regarding his determination to leave his parents' home after watching King's emotional performance, Santana later explained:

> You can't play at life unless you live it. I'm not saying you have

The Grateful Dead, pictured here in 1976, was one of several bands that were part of the San Francisco Sound—a music movement that grew out of the hippie culture of the city's Haight-Ashbury neighborhood. Clockwise from left are Bob Weir, Bill Kreutzmann, Donna Godchaux, Mickey Hart, Keith Godchaux, Phil Lesh, and Jerry Garcia.

to suffer, but you can't play the blues eating home cooking and getting your clothes washed. You have to leave your nest in order to fly. You might fall on your face, but you have to try. How can I convince anyone that my music is true if I'm still living with momma? Firsthand experience is firsthand experience. . . .You have to go out and get it.[54]

One day shortly after the King concert, Santana was working at the Tick-Tock when the Grateful Dead pulled up to the diner in two big limousines. By this time, the band was not only one of San Francisco's premier rock groups but was also well on its way to becoming a national phenomenon. All of Carlos' pent-up ambition rose within him as he watched the Grateful Dead that day. "I had my apron on," Santana recalled, "and they came over to the counter asking for french fries and burgers. I never talked to the Dead that day, I just looked at them. But something in me said, 'Man, you can do that.'"[55] He quit that very afternoon. At the age of nineteen, Carlos was ready to devote himself full time to his musical career.

HEADLINING THE FILLMORE WEST

During the course of the following year, Santana's unique Latin-, blues-, and jazz-tinged rock music attracted a large and enthusiastic following in the Bay Area. Probably the group's most devoted fan, however, was Bill Graham. "You guys have got something different," Graham told Carlos: "Your music is two things that should never be separated: spiritual and sensual."[56] Determined to do all he could to help the group, Graham secured rehearsal facilities for the band and frequently asked them to open for big-name acts at the Fillmore.

By the summer of 1968, Santana had become one of San Francisco's hottest musical acts. In recognition of the group's popularity, Graham invited Santana to headline his brand-new San Francisco concert hall, the Fillmore West (formerly the Carousel Ballroom). On June 16, 1968, Santana became the first band ever to headline at one of Graham's concert venues without having already released an album.

Three months later, Carlos Santana made his recording debut when he was asked to replace one of his guitar idols, Michael Bloomfield, on an album Mike was cutting with keyboardist Al Kooper. The album was supposed to be recorded before a live audience at the Fillmore West over the course of three evenings. On the final day of the recording session, however, Bloomfield's chronic insomnia finally got the better of him and he checked himself into a hospital. Thanks to Bill Graham, who had personally recommended him to Kooper, Carlos was one of several musicians invited to substitute for

Bloomfield. Carlos joined the keyboardist on a blues piece titled "Sonny Boy Williamson," which was later included on the album, *The Live Adventures of Mike Bloomfield and Al Kooper.*

As it turned out, the album, which was released in February 1969, was not an outstanding success, either commercially or critically. Nonetheless, 1969 would prove to be a watershed year for Carlos Santana. Although they could hardly have imagined it when the year began, by the end of that year the Mexican-American guitarist and his bandmates would be national celebrities with a best-selling and highly acclaimed album of their own.

Fame

By 1969, Santana's large following in San Francisco and unique mixture of rock, jazz, blues, and Latin rhythms had attracted the attention of several major U.S. record companies. The band decided to sign with Columbia Records and Columbia producer David Rubinson, a longtime Latin music fan, was given the task of overseeing the band's debut album.

A RECORDING DISASTER

Santana's first stab at making an album was an unqualified disaster. The long, rambling improvisations that were the hallmark of their live performances simply would not work on an album, Bill Graham had cautioned the group. "You know, if you're gonna make a record, you guys don't really have any songs, just jams, like seventeen-minute things," Carlos remembered the promoter telling the band shortly after they signed with Columbia: "'Isn't that cool,' we

Santana's first studio session during the winter of 1969 was an unqualified disaster: their songs were too long, they could not match the intensity
of playing live, and some band members were letting their personal lives
affect their performance. Pictured here are Carlos (right), Bill Graham
(center), and an unidentified man in 1981, when the band's recording
sessions proved more fruitful.

said. 'No it's not,' he said. 'You have to have some songs.'"[57]
Buoyed by their success on the San Francisco club circuit,
Carlos and his bandmates failed to take Graham's warning
seriously.

Early in the winter of 1969, the band headed to Los
Angeles for a ten-day recording session. From the start, the
project was plagued by problems. Like Graham, David
Rubinson thought the group needed to pare down its lengthy,
wandering jams into snappier, radio-friendly pieces with clear

beginnings, middles, and ends. Yet the band was no more willing to listen to the record producer than they had been to Graham. Rubinson was also disappointed by the half-hearted performances he was hearing in the Los Angeles studio; even Carlos, who was known for his fiery guitar solos, sounded oddly flat and lifeless. The band just could not seem to capture the intensity of its live performances in a recording studio.

Serious personnel troubles in the band further hindered the project. Drummer Doc Livingston had always been a heavy drinker. Recently, however, Livingston's binge drinking had been taking more and more of a toll on his performance. Livingston had been so intoxicated at Santana's New Year's Eve concert at the Winterland Arena in San Francisco that he fell off his drum kit midway through the band's performance. All too often, Livingston arrived at the Los Angeles recording sessions with a hangover and his drumming was sloppy and uninspired. Conga player Marcus Malone was also proving a liability. Just days before the recording session was scheduled to begin, Malone was arrested for stabbing his girlfriend's estranged husband after an argument erupted between the two men at the woman's apartment. Although Malone was soon released on bail, he was absent for most of the band's rehearsals. When he did show up, he was invariably distracted and short-tempered.

A NEW LINEUP AND A NEW SOUND

After spending ten dispiriting and ultimately fruitless days at the Los Angeles studio, Carlos, Rolie, and bass guitarist David Brown returned home to San Francisco convinced that drastic changes would have to be made in the Santana lineup. Malone and Livingston were promptly fired and Michael Shrieve, a talented musician with a strong background in jazz, was recruited as the band's new drummer. Shortly afterward, the band's former conga player Michael Carabello was invited back to replace Malone. The group obtained a sixth member when Carabello introduced them to José Areas, an outstanding Latin percussionist whom Michael knew from the Mission District.

Areas, who stood just five feet tall, generally went by his nickname—"Chepitó"—the chipmunk. A native of the Central American country of Nicaragua, Areas was a remarkably versatile performer. Chepitó excelled at playing several instruments, including the conga drums and the bongo, but his first love was the timbales. Of Afro-Cuban origin, the bongo is a pair of small, barrel-shaped drums of different sizes that are joined together. Played with the bare hands, it is an essential component of Latin percussion. The timbales are also heavily used in classic Latin percussion. The bandleader, composer, and percussionist Tito Puente introduced the timbales to the United States during the early 1950s, when the mambo, an Afro-Cuban style of dance music, was all the rage. Played with dowel-like sticks, the tight-skinned, shallow drums have a distinctive high-pitched tone. Typically, timbales are mounted on a stand to which cymbals and cowbells are attached as well.

By May 1969, the new and improved Santana band was ready to return to the recording studio. Everyone agreed that Shrieve's skillful drumming combined with Areas' energetic timbale playing had brought a new sophistication and richness to the group's sound. The band also had some exciting new material, including a song that Bill Graham had introduced to them entitled "Evil Ways." Composed by the Puerto Rican-American percussionist Willie Bobo, "Evil Ways" was a vibrant blend of Latin rhythms and R&B that seemed sure to receive radio play. Another standout was "Jingo," Santana's arrangement of a song by Nigerian master drummer Babatunde Olatunji.

In just three weeks, Santana managed to put together an album that pleased not only the band itself but also the executives at Columbia. Determined to heed Graham's advice this time around, the band rearranged most of its pieces into tighter, more radio-friendly songs. Titled simply *Santana*, the album was scheduled to hit the stores in October 1969.

Woodstock

Although he was not officially the group's manager—Carlos' old friend Stan Marcum retained that title—Bill Graham was unquestionably Santana's most dedicated booster. When he heard that a huge outdoor rock concert was being planned for the summer of 1969 in upstate New York, Graham was determined that his favorite San Francisco band should take part in it. The national exposure that Santana was bound to receive at the heavily hyped music festival would be invaluable to the group, he realized.

The Woodstock Music and Art Fair, as the mammoth outdoor concert was formally called, was scheduled for Friday through Sunday, August 15 to 17. Saturday evening's show was to feature the Jefferson Airplane, the Grateful Dead, and other leading rock groups from the San Francisco area. Bill Graham, who managed several of the city's most popular bands, including the Jefferson Airplane, tried to persuade the concert's promoters to sign Santana as well. At first the promoters balked at Graham's request, arguing that few people outside of California had ever heard of the band. But when Graham implied that he would pull some of the big-name acts he represented from the concert if Santana did not perform, they caved.

Although the festival was named for the town of Woodstock, an artists' mecca about 100 miles from New York City, Woodstock proper could not accommodate such a large event. Consequently, the actual concert site was several miles away from Woodstock, just outside the small town of Bethel. Fortunately for the concert's organizers, the owner of one of the largest farms in the area agreed to rent out 600 acres of land to them for the three-day event.

Late on the morning of August 16, Santana was flown to

the concert site by helicopter—the only way the band could get into the festival at that point. The organizers had expected a crowd of 60,000; instead, nearly 500,000 young people from throughout the country descended on the tiny community of Bethel to hear Jimi Hendrix, The Who, Sly and the Family Stone, and other superstar acts perform at what was being billed as the greatest rock concert in history. By the time the festival had officially opened on Friday evening, a flood of young concert-goers had clogged all of the roads leading into Bethel for miles and brought traffic on the nearby New York State Thruway to a standstill.

A Show-Stopping Performance

When the Santana band arrived at the concert venue about 12:00 P.M., they assumed they would not play for another seven or eight hours. To pass the time, Carlos decided to take a tablet of mescaline, a potent psychedelic. He was confident that the drug would wear off by the time he had to perform. Ever since Stan Marcum had introduced him to the hippie culture of Haight-Ashbury in the mid-1960s, Carlos had been an enthusiastic user of hallucinogens. In those days, the young guitarist had an almost religious zeal for psychedelics, viewing them as a means of achieving greater self-knowledge and spiritual enlightenment: "I felt [the drugs] would make it more real and honest," he revealed to *Rolling Stone* in 2000. "I don't recommend it to anybody and everybody, yet for me I felt [taking psychedelics] did wonders. It made me aware of splendor and rapture."[58]

Not "splendor and rapture" but raw terror was what Carlos was feeling after he swallowed the mescaline that August afternoon, however. Just as the drug was starting to take effect, Carlos was informed that the band would have to go on immediately. After a long night of driving rain followed by a brutally hot and humid morning, the hundreds of thousands of high school and college students who had jammed into the concert site's muddy pastures and fields were cranky and impatient.

On August 16, 1969, Santana performed at the Woodstock Music and Art Fair in Bethel, New York, captivating audiences with its performance of "Soul Sacrifice." Pictured here at Woodstock from left are Carlos Santana, timbalero José Areas, percussionist Michael Carabello, drummer Michael Shrieve (foreground), and bassist David Brown.

Worried that the restive crowd might riot if the entertainment on stage stopped for long, Woodstock's organizers had persuaded the evening's top performers to play longer sets than had been originally scheduled. That meant that lesser-known acts like Santana could be moved up to the afternoon to ensure that the music would continue throughout the day and well into the night.

As the band members took their positions on stage, Carlos peered out at the vast audience and in his drugged state saw an alarming "ocean of flesh and hair and teeth and hands. . . . I just prayed that the Lord would keep me in tune and in time."[59] During the first part of the group's hour-long set, all but overwhelmed by the potent dose of mescaline he had ingested, Carlos struggled mightily to focus on the music. "When I see it on TV, it's like another guy playing," he says of the concert today. "He was trying to get in there, dealing with the electric snake. Instead of a guitar neck, [he] was playing with an electric snake."[60] Not until the final song of the set, a long and fiery instrumental jam called "Soul Sacrifice," did Carlos finally feel back in control of his thoughts and body.

As it turned out, the band's performance of "Soul Sacrifice" would be one of the festival's highlights. The exotic Latin rhythms of the piece combined with Carlos' blistering performance on the guitar electrified the crowd. Never before had they seen anything like this multiracial band with its white drummer and keyboardist, black bass guitarist, and Latino guitarist and percussionist. Nor had they ever heard anything quite like Santana's searing hybrid of rock, jazz, blues, and Latin music. By the end of the nearly ten-minute-long jam, the crowd was on its feet, cheering wildly and Santana had been catapulted to instant stardom.

Santana Takes Off

Released in the wake of the band's heavily publicized performance at Woodstock, the album *Santana* was an immediate hit. Record-buyers and critics alike were enthralled by the group's adventurous, Latin-spiked music. In an age when rock fans idolized guitar virtuosos like Jimi Hendrix and Eric Clapton, it was inevitable that Santana's fiery lead guitarist should soon emerge as the group's brightest star. Carlos' passionate, high-pitched solos, and particularly his penchant for sustaining single notes on his Gibson guitar for astonishingly long periods, mesmerized listeners. It was evident from the start that the skinny Mexican-American guitarist had a style all his own: "Guitar was unknown, voiced the way it was in Santana,"[61] notes David Rubinson of Columbia Records.

By early 1970, *Santana* had already produced a Top-10 single, "Evil Ways," and was well on its way to achieving double-platinum status. (Records are said to "go platinum" after one million units are sold.) That spring, the band received another boost when the documentary film *Woodstock* and an accompanying soundtrack album were released. Initially, the film's producers offered the band $750 to use its performance of "Soul Sacrifice" in the movie. Bill Graham was outraged by this stingy offer and let the producers know it: "The footage they had on Santana was *magic*. I said, 'You want to use this, there's a price. You know it's going to be a hit. You don't want to pay the price. Don't use it.'"[62] Graham eventually convinced the producers to pay Santana $35,000 to use "Soul Sacrifice" in the film, an amount nearly 50 times greater than their original offer.

As the *Woodstock* album climbed to the top of the *Billboard* charts, Santana embarked on its first international tour after

THE DISASTROUS ALTAMONT MUSIC FESTIVAL

On December 6, 1969, less than four months after their triumphant appearance at the Woodstock Music and Art Fair in New York, the Santana band played at another large and highly publicized outdoor rock concert, this time on the West Coast. Held at Altamont Speedway, just a few miles from the band's hometown of San Francisco, the violence-ridden Altamont Music Festival would stand in stark contrast to gentle-spirited Woodstock, the so-called festival of love and peace.

The violence that marred Altamont might have been avoided if the concert's organizers, the British supergroup the Rolling Stones, had not taken the advice of their friends in the Grateful Dead and enlisted several local chapters of the Hell's Angels motorcycle gang to provide security for the free event. According to some accounts, the Stones offered more than 300 of the outlaw bikers hundreds of dollars worth of beer and other alcoholic beverages in return for policing the concert.

Santana was the first band to play that December day at the Altamont Speedway. During their final number, the group was shocked to see a fan being chased across the stage by several of six months of nearly nonstop touring in the United States. Designed to coincide with the release of *Santana* overseas, the sold-out concert tour took the band to Denmark, Germany, and England and culminated with an appearance at the celebrated Montreux Jazz Festival in Switzerland.

A Number One Album

By the summer of 1970, the band was beginning to formulate plans for a second album, *Abraxas*. Rolie convinced his bandmates to include the sensuous blues-rock song, "Black Magic Woman," by British composer Peter Green on the new record. At Carlos' insistence, Tito Puente's catchy Afro-Cuban song,

(*continued on page 68*)

the hired thugs. To the horror of Carlos and his bandmates, the beer-swilling bikers soon caught up with their quarry and began beating the terrified young man to a bloody pulp. As the day wore on, the violence only escalated. By the end of the concert, the out-of-control "security" guards had severely injured dozens of concert-goers and killed one, an 18-year-old Afro-American man named Meredith Hunter. As the Rolling Stones performed onstage just a few feet away, several Hell's Angels stabbed, clubbed, and kicked Hunter to death.

The hostility and violence that marred the Altamont Music Festival "helped to dash the sense of innocence and optimism engendered at Woodstock,"* writes historian Edward Rielly in his book *The 1960s*. After that tragic day at the San Francisco raceway, the belief that massive free rock concerts in the tradition of Woodstock could somehow promote harmony and love among the nation's people began to seem painfully naïve to many Americans, young and old alike.

*   Edward Rielly, *The 1960's* (Westport, Conn., Greenwood Press, 2003), 211.

A ROLE MODEL FOR EVERYONE

For nearly four decades, Hispanics have been looking up to Carlos Santana. For many Chicanos and other Latinos, the critically acclaimed musician and philanthropist from the little Mexican village of Autlán de Navarro has come to represent what can be achieved as a Latin immigrant in the United States.

Over the years, Carlos Santana's importance as a positive role model for Americans of Latin descent has been recognized time and time again in the form of honors and awards from a host of Hispanic political, cultural, and community organizations. In 1991, for example, the California State Latino Legislative Caucus passed an official resolution recognizing Carlos' extraordinary contributions to the arts and unwavering commitment to the Latino community. Eight years later, the Hispanic Congressional Caucus presented the guitarist-songwriter with the Medallion of Excellence Award for Community Service. In 1999, Santana was also honored with the Alma Award for Special Achievement by the National Council of La Raza, a Washington D.C.-based Latino advocacy organization. *Hispanic* magazine bestowed its Life Achievement Award on Santana in 2000, and in 2001 the Mexican-American icon and his wife Deborah King Santana received the Second Annual César E. Chávez Spirit Award. Presented by the University of California–Los Angeles, the César E. Chávez Spirit Award honors those Americans who continue to pursue the late union organizer and civil rights leader's vision of social justice.

Carlos' lofty standing among the Hispanic community in the United States, and particularly on the West Coast, where he and his wife still make their home today, was especially evident in 1987 when the city of San Francisco officially declared June 6 as Santana Day in recognition of Carlos' many civic and cultural contributions to the Bay Area. The highlight of the day was a free Santana concert in the guitarist's old neighborhood, the city's predominantly Latino Mission District. To coincide with the celebration, San Francisco artist Michael Rios painted a huge wall mural of Carlos and the legendary Latin-American percussionists Eddie Palmieri and Armando Peraza in the heart of the Mission District.

Carlos Santana is also an icon for millions of Hispanics outside of the United States. Carlos and the Santana band have visited Latin America many times since the group first became an international phenomenon in 1969. Wherever he performs, Carlos is invariably greeted by huge and adoring crowds. As Simon Leng notes in his biography of Santana, Carlos' impoverished childhood in rural Mexico and gritty story of street survival in Tijuana have only served to enhance his larger-than-life image for many Latin Americans. In 1992, when Carlos returned to Tijuana for one of the most emotional performances of his career—a "regresa a casa" (homecoming) concert at the city's giant seaside bullring—an ecstatic crowd of nearly 20,000 greeted the guitarist-songwriter like a returning hero.

Carlos Santana has repeatedly stated that he wants to be viewed first and foremost as a citizen of the world and not as a Mexican American. Nevertheless, over the years Santana has come to accept that he is a highly visible role model for other Hispanics and has striven to set a positive example in both his career and his personal life. "I want to be part of a positive change for Latins," he told *Billboard* magazine in 2004. "I value how I present myself. Integrity is not something you can buy in Rodeo Drive or the most expensive boutiques in Miami. It's a dress they don't sell in those places. Integrity is a garment you can achieve by walking hand in hand with God."

Although Santana hopes to bring his message of moral responsibility and spiritual growth to all his listeners around the globe, in recent years he has become increasingly concerned with sharing that message with his fellow Latinos. Education is critical to breaking the cycles of poverty, violence, and despair that afflict far too many Hispanic communities today, he maintains. This educational program must emphasize Hispanic history and culture in order to instill pride in young people, he asserts, as well as spiritual instruction to help them learn how to transform negative and potentially destructive emotions and energies into positive, uplifting ones. As Santana told Leila Cobo of *Billboard* magazine in 2004, he is particularly drawn to the late César Chávez's famous rallying cry, "Sí se puede" ("Yes, we can.") That is "the only agenda worth being passionate about," the musician and philanthropist insists. "Everything else usually comes down to a very shallow thing."

(*continued from page 65*)
"Oye Como Va," was also included. Rico Reyes, an acquaintance of the band from the Mission District, was hired to sing the lyrics to Puente's tangy salsa piece in Spanish.

Santana's second album was an even bigger hit than its first. Following the record's release in October, *Abraxas* was the number 1 album in the United States for six weeks and yielded two Top-10 singles in the band's Latin-flavored rendition of "Black Magic Woman" and joyful cover of "Oye Como Va." Eventually, more than four million copies of the critically acclaimed album would be sold throughout the world.

Abraxas was an unqualified success for the band, commercially and artistically. Yet by the time the album was released in late 1970, Santana had already begun to disintegrate. Just one year after Santana's show-stopping performance at the Woodstock festival, escalating drug use and internal power struggles were threatening to tear the band apart.

A Troubled Band

Although he was still using psychedelics on a regular basis, Carlos was concerned by the growing dependence of several of his bandmates, and especially Michael Carabello and David Brown, on hard drugs such as cocaine and heroin. During the fall of 1970, two of the rock world's brightest young stars, Jimi Hendrix and Janice Joplin, died within weeks of each other of drug overdoses. Yet, to Carlos' dismay, Hendrix and Joplin's untimely deaths did not seem to faze Santana's high-living members. By the beginning of 1971, cocaine and heroin use had become so rampant within the band that Carlos was worried about the group's ability to perform in public. Years later, he recalled a recurring nightmare from this very stressful period in his life. In the dream, Santana had been invited to perform before a huge audience, but Carlos' bandmates were so high on drugs that they could not play a single note.

José Areas, pictured here in 1988 at the North Sea Jazz Festival in the Netherlands, was an original member of Santana. The talented percussionist from San Francisco's Mission District was nicknamed Chepitó due to his small stature.

In February 1971, the troubled band received a major blow when its talented percussionist Chepitó Areas suffered a ruptured aneurysm in his brain. It looked as though Areas would have to spend at least six months in the hospital recovering from the burst blood vessel, and there was a real possibility that he might never be able to perform again. That winter, the band was scheduled to play at a major concert in Ghana, Africa, and tour Europe for a second time. Michael Carabello, never shy about expressing his opinions, was adamant that the band should cancel all its engagements until Areas recovered. "Chepitó's just as much a part of the band as anyone else," Carabello argued. "I don't think we should get another person to fill his place and go before an audience and say this is Santana, because we're not."[63] Carlos, on the other hand, was equally determined that the group should fulfill all its commitments. In the end, Carlos prevailed and the band, accompanied by a succession of substitute percussionists, performed in Ghana and a number of European cities, including London, Milan, and Paris. In the wake of their bitter squabble over Areas, however, relations between Carabello and Carlos Santana were permanently strained.

During the tour, Carlos also butted heads with his bandmates, including longtime member Greg Rolie, over the addition of percussionist Coke Escovedo to the group. After joining up with Santana in London, the timbale player quickly became Carlos' closest ally and confidante, and the other band members suspected Escovedo of trying to turn Carlos against them. In fact, Escovedo probably had little impact on Carlos' attitude toward the rest of the band. By the time Coke had arrived on the scene, Carlos was already thoroughly disgusted with what he viewed as his bandmates' shallow preoccupation with the "rock 'n' roll lifestyle" of hard drugs, alcohol, and casual sex and their steadily declining interest in the music itself. "I was starting to feel weak and resentful towards the band," Carlos would later admit. "I was demanding more because my soul was demanding more."[64]

A New Album and the End of the Fillmore West

During the summer of 1971, the band members put aside their differences to record their third album, *Santana III*. In all, twelve musicians played on the album, including teenage guitar virtuoso Neal Schon, whom Rolie and Shrieve had recruited for the band six months earlier, percussionist Coke Escovedo, singer Rico Reyes, trumpeter Luis Gasca, and pianist Mario Ochoa. Chepitó Areas, who had made a miraculous recovery from his ruptured aneurysm, also lent his considerable talents to the project.

Santana III, considered by some critics as the group's finest recording, had a noticeably stronger Latin flavor than the band's first two albums. The album includes two full-fledged salsa pieces: Tito Puente's "Para Los Rumberos," featuring the mariachi-style trumpet playing of Luis Gasca, and the song "Guajira," featuring Spanish lyrics and a classic cha-cha-cha rhythm. The fiery rock instrumental "Toussaint L'Overture" is based on a traditional Spanish guitar chord pattern, and like most of the tracks on the album, is fueled by Areas, Carabello, and Escovedo's energetic Latin percussion.

Shortly after completing *Santana III*, the original Woodstock lineup of Carlos Santana, Gregg Rolie, Michael Shrieve, Michael Carabello, Chepitó Areas, and David Brown, augmented by guitarist Schon and percussionist Escovedo, made what would be their final public appearance as a cohesive unit at the closing of the Fillmore West. The band had agreed to perform at the Fourth of July show as a special favor to their friend and mentor, Bill Graham. After their set was over, the band joined musicians from Creedence Clearwater Revival, Tower of Power, and other leading San Francisco groups for a huge, all-night jam session in honor of the man who had done so much to promote their careers.

Breakup

The Fillmore West concert was an unqualified success for Santana; the group's spirited performance was generally considered the highlight of the entire event. Nonetheless, Carlos was growing increasingly disenchanted with the band. By the late summer of 1971, he was going out of his way to minimize his contact with his bandmates, even skipping rehearsals for the group's upcoming U.S. tour to promote the soon-to-be released *Santana III* album. The chief focal point of Carlos' discontent was Michael Carabello, a heavy cocaine user and confirmed womanizer whom Santana blamed more than anyone else for the band's increasing absorption in the seamier side of the rock 'n' roll lifestyle. He particularly detested the shady characters who always seemed to be hanging around the conga player whenever the band went on tour. Carlos recalled going down to the hotel lobby after one concert to see what was happening only to find it "full of pimps, dealers, and weirdos. It was like walking into a swamp."[65] "[Carlos] like had this thing about me," Carabello mused years later: "The people I hung around with, what I did, how I ran my life."[66]

Just as the band was preparing to embark on its U.S. tour, Carlos presented his bandmates with an ultimatum: either Carabello was out or he was out. Offended by what they considered Carlos' strong-arm tactics, the rest of the group voted to go ahead without their lead guitarist. Santana's first show in Boston went well enough with Neal Schon filling in for Carlos, but at the band's next stop in Washington, D.C., the crowd repeatedly called out for Carlos and 16-year-old Schon was thoroughly unnerved. When Carabello announced he was bowing out of the tour before the band's next big concert in New York City, Stan Marcum and Chepitó Areas loyally followed the conga player. On hearing the news, Carlos immediately flew to New York, where he was greeted by an angry Gregg Rolie. Rolie told the guitarist that he was willing to stay on for the remainder of the tour but that he wanted as little to do with Carlos as possible. "I'll play," Rolie told Santana. "But don't look at me. Don't talk to me."[67]

After securing a substitute percussionist, Santana managed to hobble through the rest of the band's U.S. tour, finishing out 1971 with concerts in Puerto Rico and Lima, Peru. But Carlos was more discouraged than ever about the group's future. Even the news that the recently released *Santana III* had risen to the top of the album charts failed to cheer him. "Carlos Santana felt that he was at a dead end, musically, spiritually, and physically,"[68] writes his biographer Simon Leng. By the beginning of

1972, Carlos had made a crucial decision: he had resolved to officially take back his name from Santana and make the band his own.

6

New Directions

Following the breakup of the original Santana band in 1972, Carlos Santana sought out new musical and spiritual paths. He turned away from his Catholic roots to explore Eastern religions and put aside his blues and R&B records to listen to cutting-edge jazz artists like trumpeter Miles Davis, saxophonist John Coltrane, and guitarist John McLaughlin.

CARAVANSERAI

A few months after his takeover of the group, Carlos began recording the first Santana album without the old Woodstock-era lineup. Carlos' coproducer for *Caravanserai*, as the new album was titled, was Michael Shrieve, the sole band member to whom Carlos had remained close following the breakup. Shrieve shared Carlos' devotion to jazz and particularly a bold new type of jazz called fusion. A hybrid of jazz and rock, fusion combines the complexity and improvisational freedom of jazz with the driving rhythms and

74

electronic amplification of rock and roll. Two other members of the original band, Gregg Rolie and Neal Schon, supplied keyboard and guitar parts for several tracks on *Caravanserai* but did not participate in the planning and production of the album. By this time, Rolie and Schon had already resolved to form their own rock group, Journey. In all, sixteen different musicians contributed their talents to *Caravanserai*, including bass guitarist Doug Rauch, keyboard player Tom Coster, and Latin percussionist virtuoso Armando Peraza.

Caravanserai had little in common with Santana's previous albums. Almost entirely instrumental, the record features a jazzy, dreamy style that reflected Carlos' new interest in fusion, as well as his growing fascination with Eastern spirituality. Clive Davis, the president of Columbia Records, was troubled by the direction that Carlos and his reconstituted band were taking. Because the album lacked any radio-friendly songs, it was almost certain to be a commercial failure, Davis fretted. When Davis warned him that he was "committing career suicide" by making *Caravanserai*, however, Carlos insisted that he would not give up his artistic vision in order to pander to the marketplace: "I actually know you're saying this from your heart," he told the worried record executive, "but I've gotta do this."[69]

Although *Caravanserai* failed to match the phenomenal success of the first three Santana albums, to the delight of Davis and his associates at Columbia, it reached number eight on the national album charts after receiving glowing reviews in *Rolling Stone* and other popular American music publications. Davis was further heartened by the success of Santana's European tour to promote the new album. Some fans were clearly disappointed by Carlos' decision to focus on the free-flowing jazz fusion of *Caravanserai* while all but ignoring classic Santana hits such as "Evil Ways" and "Black Magic Woman." Nevertheless, the concerts were well attended and the European press was overwhelmingly positive regarding Santana's new, more sophisticated sound. *(continued on page 78)*

A CIRCLE OF FRIENDS

FAMOUS MUSICIANS INSPIRE CARLOS SANTANA

Over the course of his long and eclectic career, Carlos Santana has developed close professional and personal relationships with leading performers from many different nations and genres of music. His circle of famous musician friends and collaborators has included British rock star Eric Clapton, African guitar virtuoso Salif Keita, Mississippi bluesman John Lee Hooker, Brazilian singer and songwriter Milton Nascimento, and Hungarian jazz master Gabor Szabo.

Santana's friendships with some of the world's foremost jazz artists have been particularly significant in his evolution as a musician. During the 1970s and 1980s as his own interest in jazz was blossoming, Santana became close to many of the most respected jazz musicians of his time, including drummer-guitarist Buddy Miles, his collaborator on several recording projects; pianist-composer Herbie Hancock, his collaborator on the critically acclaimed album *Swing of Delight*; and saxophonist-composer Wayne Shorter, his partner on a memorable tour of the European jazz festivals in 1988.

Among his numerous friendships with jazz artists, however, the relationship that Carlos Santana valued above all others was with the late trumpeter, bandleader, and composer, Miles Davis. Born in Alton, Illinois, in 1926, Davis started playing the trumpet at the age of 10. In 1944, when he was 18, Davis moved to New York City to be near his idol, jazz saxophonist Charlie Parker. By the late 1940s, the young trumpeter was already leading his own ensemble. During the following decade, Davis would emerge as the most consistently original musician in American jazz, helping to found both the understated "cool jazz" genre and the controversial "modal jazz" style, which features no chord changes.

Inspired by the Afro-American rock stars Jimi Hendrix and James Brown, by the late 1960s Davis had begun experimenting with fusion, a jazz-rock hybrid that would have an enormous impact on many of his contemporaries, including British guitarist John McLaughlin and the young Carlos Santana. Deeply impressed by Davis' groundbreaking fusion album of 1969 entitled *Bitches Brew*, Carlos was thrilled when the trumpeter agreed to open for the Santana band on its first post-Woodstock tour of the United States. During the tour, Carlos and Davis became close friends, and by the early 1970s Santana was incorporating Davis' innovative fusion style in his own work. Davis, in turn, inspired by Santana's unique blending of Latin percussion with rock, soon added congas and timbales to his jazz ensemble.

Over the years, another key component of Carlos Santana's inner circle has been his many friends from the Latin music world. Early in his recording and performing career, Carlos developed close relationships with some of the greatest figures in Latin American music, including bandleaders and composers Eddie Palmieri, Ray Baretto, and Willie Bobo; bongo and conga virtuoso Armando Peraza; and "the King" ("El Rey") of Latin music—composer, bandleader, and timbales master, Tito Puente. These superstars of Latin jazz and pop were among Carlos' earliest fans, and during the 1960s, their outspoken support for Santana's revolutionary fusion of Latin rhythms and percussion with rock and roll played a key role in the band's acceptance by the more traditional elements within the Latin music community.

By the 1990s, Carlos Santana had befriended a new generation of Latino musicians who had been deeply influenced by his unprecedented mixing of Latin, blues, jazz, and rock. Among the best known of these younger musicians are the Los Angeles band Ozomatli, which specializes in a distinctive blend of rock, salsa, hip-hop, jazz, and funk, and the popular Tex-Mex rock group Los Lonely Boys. Both bands have toured with Santana, and Los Lonely Boys recently recorded a song with Carlos for his third album with record producer Clive Davis. Guitarist Henry Garza of Los Lonely Boys considers Carlos one of his most important musical role models and mentors: "[Santana's] music was something new, but it was intertwined with everything else that was out there at the time—Sixties rock, Latin jazz and more," Garza told *Rolling Stone* magazine in 2005. "We're trying to do the same thing with Los Lonely Boys—make a lot of different types of music into something our own—but he did that first. He incorporated his culture into the music, and he mixed English and Spanish in the lyrics. . . . He's a pioneer of Latin rock & roll."

Carlos Santana and Deborah King met at a concert at the Marin Civic Center in San Rafael, California, in 1972. The couple, pictured here at the Bay Area Music Awards in 1981, have been married for thirty-two years and have three children.

(continued from page 75)

CARLOS AND DEBORAH

Despite the critical and commercial success of his new album and band, Carlos felt dissatisfied and depressed. "A lot of people may not know it, but the more successful you are . . . the more lonely it gets, because when you see people coming and approaching you, you know they're approaching you with different intentions than someone who knows you,"[70] Carlos later explained. "I had platinum albums in my house, drugs, food, flesh, and all those kinds of things. But I felt such an emptiness. Everything felt dead to me,"[71] he recalled. Then, during the summer of 1972 at a concert at the Marin Civic Center just across the bay from San Francisco, Carlos' life changed forever when he met the woman who was to become his soul mate and lifelong companion, Deborah King.

The daughter of Saunders King, a pioneering electric blues guitarist, Deborah was a 22-year-old student at San Francisco State College when she and 25-year-old Carlos Santana first encountered one another at the Marin Civic Center. Deborah had just ended a romantic relationship with rock star Sylvester (Sly) Stone and, like Carlos, was thoroughly disillusioned with the freewheeling rock 'n' roll lifestyle. Also in common with Carlos, Deborah had recently begun to explore Eastern religions and meditation in an effort to find a greater sense of meaning and purpose for her life. By the end of their first date, Carlos was head over heels in love with this intelligent and intensely spiritual young woman. Following a whirlwind, eight-month-long courtship, Deborah and Carlos were married on April 20, 1973, in a modest ceremony in the Bay area home of Deborah's uncle.

Sri Chinmoy

By the time of their marriage in the spring of 1973, Deborah and Carlos had already become deeply involved with a man who was to have a dramatic impact on their personal and professional lives for nearly a decade: the Indian philosopher and guru (religious teacher) Sri Chinmoy.

Born in Bangladesh in 1931, in the mid-1960s Chinmoy moved to New York City, where he would serve as an interfaith chaplain at the United Nations for many years. His teachings emphasized meditation, acts of physical endurance such as long-distance running and weight lifting, and abstinence from drugs, tobacco, and alcohol. During the early 1970s, Chinmoy counted several well-known musicians among his followers, including guitarist John McLaughlin of the British jazz fusion group the Mahavishnu Orchestra. It was McLaughlin who first introduced Carlos to Chinmoy after Santana traveled to New York to discuss a possible musical collaboration with the jazz guitarist.

Carlos was immediately drawn to Chinmoy's teachings and particularly his insistence that the power of love must replace the love of power in human relations. Within weeks of meeting the charismatic guru, he and Deborah had decided to join Chinmoy's interfaith group, which operated a large meditation center in their hometown of San Francisco.

The couple had committed themselves to a stern regimen. Santana was ordered to cut off his long, curly hair and wear only white clothing as a constant reminder to keep his mind and body pure. Deborah, like all the guru's female disciples, was expected to dress in flowing saris, the traditional garb of Hindu women in India. Both Carlos and Deborah were given new spiritual names by Chinmoy: Carlos was henceforth to be known as Devadip (meaning, "the Lamp, the Eye, the Light of God") and Deborah as Urmila ("the Light of the Supreme"). Every day the Santanas awoke at 5:00 A.M. for half an hour of meditation following by an additional 30 minutes of studying Chinmoy's books and poetry. At the guru's urging, the couple became strict vegetarians, gave up all drugs and alcohol, and started running marathons: "It was like a West Point approach to spirituality,"[72] Santana would later muse.

"Music to Inspire the Soul"

During the first several years after joining Chinmoy's group, Carlos dedicated himself to creating music that reflected and reinforced his guru's spiritual teachings: "music to inspire the soul, to uplift the consciousness of humanity,"[73] as Santana put it. In 1973, Carlos collaborated on the album *Love, Devotion and Surrender*—named after one of Chinmoy's religious poems—with fellow spiritual seeker and jazz fusion enthusiast John McLaughlin. That same year, Carlos and the Santana band, which still included two members of the old group—drummer Michael Shrieve and percussionist Chepitó Areas—recorded *Welcome*, a collection of contemplative, jazz-oriented songs with lyrics based on Sri Chinmoy's meditations. Then in 1974, Carlos collaborated with harpist and organist Alice Coltrane, another Chinmoy disciple and the widow of jazz legend John Coltrane, on *Illuminations*, an Indian-influenced, entirely instrumental album.

Carlos' Chinmoy-inspired albums failed to generate much enthusiasm among Santana's fan base, particularly in the United States. The records also received mixed reviews from American critics, although the European music press was generally positive regarding Santana's new direction. From a commercial standpoint, *Love, Devotion and Surrender* did the best of the three albums, making it into the Top 20 on the national charts. *Welcome*, however, never went beyond number 25 on the charts, and *Illuminations* could not even break into the Top 40. Seemingly undeterred by the albums' obvious lack of commercial appeal, Carlos hit the road with a concert program based largely on music from *Love, Devotion and Surrender*, *Welcome*, and *Borboletta*, a progressive, Latin-flavored jazz fusion album that he recorded with the Santana band and various guest artists in 1974. At the concerts, Carlos—or Devadip as he insisted on being called—often recited his guru's meditations as introductions to the band's songs. Some members of Santana were clearly uncomfortable with Carlos' devotion to Chinmoy and the band's personnel changed regularly throughout the 1970s. Carlos was especially disappointed when his old friend and fellow jazz buff Michael Shrieve quit the band in 1974 to pursue solo projects.

Carlos Santana did achieve one major commercial success in the mid-1970s, when *Santana's Greatest Hits* album, a collection of the old band's most popular songs from *Santana*, *Abraxas*, and *Santana III*, was released. The album, which raced up the charts following its release in August 1974, would eventually go double platinum.

Sri Chinmoy, pictured here (center) at the United Nations in 1987, where he served as interfaith chaplain for many years, was Carlos and Deborah Santana's spiritual guru from 1973 to 1981. Chinmoy advocated meditation, acts of physical endurance, and abstinence from addictive substances as ways to achieve enlightenment.

Carlos Compromises

By the end of 1974, disappointed by the low sales figures for *Barboletta* and most of Santana's other recent efforts, the executives at Columbia were putting more and more pressure on Carlos to re-embrace the band's Latin rock roots. At first, the guitarist resisted his record company's demands to produce more radio-friendly albums: "I accepted . . . that I was kissing goodbye to a lot of my so-called audience. But I felt that I didn't want to be a monkey, where someone pulled the strings and I played whatever they wanted me to play—I have a soul, and it's a crime to ignore it, so I'll pay the price whatever it is, and whatever I have to do, I'll do it,"[74] Carlos told one interviewer.

After he asked Bill Graham to serve as the band's new

manager in 1975, however, Carlos' attitude toward his record company gradually began to soften. Over the years, Graham had been like a father to Carlos, and his opinion meant a great deal to the guitarist. Consequently, Carlos listened when Graham, fearful that Columbia's executives were losing their patience with his client, counseled him to return to the classic Santana sound of the late 1960s and early 1970s on his albums with the band. He could then focus on the jazz fusion and spiritual music that he loved on his solo projects, Graham told Carlos.

At Graham's suggestion, Santana invited Columbia producer David Rubinson to oversee the band's next album. Since supervising Santana's first stab at making an album back in 1969, Rubinson had developed a reputation for turning out hit records. In late 1975, the band began recording *Amigos* under Rubinson's and Graham's direction. The album reflected both the Latin-infused blues-rock style of the Woodstock-era Santana band and a popular new kind of Afro-American music known as funk. An offshoot of soul and rhythm and blues, funk music features a repetitive, high-volume bass line and heavy syncopation.

Released in the spring of 1976, *Amigos* was an instant hit not only in the United States but also in Europe and Latin America. The executives at Columbia Records were thrilled with *Amigos'* success and rewarded the guitarist with a generous new contract. Most important to Carlos, the new contract guaranteed him the freedom to pursue his personal musical and spiritual interests on three solo albums.

Commerce and Art

A year after *Amigo* hit the markets, the Santana band released another commercially successful album, *Festival*, which featured a number of catchy, salsa-influenced songs. That same year, Santana also released *Moonflower*, a mixture of new studio material and live takes of many of the group's classic hits, including "Black Magic Woman." The band's best selling album since *Abraxas* in 1970, *Moonflower* reached number 10 on the U.S. and number 7 on the British charts, and spawned a Top-10 single, a Latin-infused cover of a 1960s song by the Zombies entitled, "She's Not There."

During the late 1970s, when he was not working on more commercial endeavors with his band, Carlos produced two solo albums that reflected his true musical and spiritual passions. Released in 1979, the album *Oneness* mirrored Carlos' wide-ranging musical interests in everything from Afro-Cuban percussion to Indian devotional songs to European classical compositions. In 1980, Carlos followed up *Oneness* with an ambitious jazz fusion album entitled *The Swing of Delight*. Carlos was thrilled when several of jazz's most respected stars, including pianist Herbie Hancock and saxophonist Wayne Shorter, agreed to play on the all-instrumental album. Although the music press loved the album, with *Downbeat* magazine even awarding it a five-star review, like *Oneness*, *The Swing of Delight* failed to make much money. Consequently, as the decade of the 1980s began, Carlos felt more pressure than ever to produce a top-selling album with his band in order to support the less commercial solo projects he cherished.

Leaving Sri Chinmoy

In the meantime, Carlos was becoming increasingly disgruntled with his longtime guru Sri Chinmoy. Deborah Santana shared her husband's growing sense of disillusionment with the couple's spiritual teacher. As Deborah explained in her memoirs, *Space Among the Stars*, although their association with Chinmoy had once brought the couple joy and a sense of belonging, they eventually came to feel that the guru was keeping them "in bondage of mind and spirit. . . . Sri Chinmoy . . . was asking us to deny thinking for ourselves so that we would do whatever he said."[75] The guru had even gone so far as to persuade Carlos and Deborah to put off starting a family because he viewed children as a distraction from the meditative life.

By the end of 1981, Carlos and Deborah had resolved to part ways with Chinmoy. To their dismay, the guru was furious when he heard that they were leaving his group. Any disciple who dared to forsake him and his teachings "could only fall into the depths of darkness." Chinmoy warned the couple: "You have twenty-four hours to change your minds or the door will be closed forever."[76]

But there was to be no turning back for the Santanas. "Carlos and I had outgrown [Chinmoy's] make-believe realm and had unbraided our mental dependency on him as our link to God," writes Deborah Santana: "We sought the God-ness that existed inside us. . . . No more 'Yes, Guru'; 'Whatever you say, Guru.' No more bowing to a frail form of divinity."[77] Yet Carlos and Deborah's decision to part ways with Chinmoy did not mean that they had abandoned their long spiritual quest. Soon after leaving Chinmoy's group, Deborah and Carlos renewed their commitment to the Christian faith in which both had been raised and became part of the evangelical "born-again" Christian movement then sweeping the United States.

Ups and Downs of the 1980s

In 1981, the same year that he broke with Sri Chinmoy, Carlos and Santana gave Columbia the hit album the company's executives had long sought when *Zebop!* broke into the *Billboard* Top-10 albums chart and produced a Top-10 single in the song "Winning." Although the highly danceable *Zebop!* was a huge commercial success for Santana, the album was panned by music critics as uninspired and blatantly commercial. *Shango*, which was released the following year, also reflected the band's move toward a more marketable sound. *Shango* produced a Top-20 hit in the song "Hold On" but left some critics wondering if Carlos had concluded that achieving success on the record charts was more important than preserving his reputation as a serious musician.

Over the next few years, Carlos released two disappointing

Santana, pictured here in 1981, when the group's album *Zebop!* reached the Billboard Top 10, experienced many ups and downs during the 1980s. By 1990, the band was disillusioned with Columbia Records and signed a new contract with Polygram Records.

albums, *Harvest Moon* and *Beyond Appearances*, both of which were critical as well as commercial flops. As a live performer, however, Carlos enjoyed far more success during the mid-1980s. In 1984, his tour of Europe with the legendary singer and songwriter Bob Dylan was well received by both his fans and the music press. Two years later, Carlos earned rave reviews for his fiery performance in a special concert with the old Santana band to mark the twentieth anniversary of the formation of the Santana Blues Band. Nearly 20 former and current members of the Santana band, including Gregg Rolie,

Chepitó Areas, and Michael Carabello, played in the three-hour show at the Shoreline Amphitheater, Bill Graham's new concert venue just outside San Francisco.

In 1987, Carlos embarked on a lengthy tour of Europe and the Middle East to promote Santana's latest album, *Freedom*, a spirited mixture of Latin rock, Afro-Cuban jazz, R&B, funk, and soul. The well-publicized *Freedom* tour was Carlos' tenth international tour with the Santana band since 1970. It would also prove to be one of the most satisfying tours of his long musical career, both professionally and personally. On the tour, Carlos and his band visited a number of places where they had never played before, including Vienna, Helsinki, East Berlin, and Budapest. The tour also included several stops in the violence-ridden Middle East. A concert in Jerusalem attended by 10,000 Jewish and Arab fans proved particularly rewarding for the guitarist: "What Carlos Santana saw was Jews and Arabs enjoying the music and getting along together, even if it was only for three hours," writes Simon Leng. "But to him that was the point, only the universal sound of music could heal these wounds. It was fitting that on this tour [the band] had started to play a moody selection that had a Spanish name, "Curandero," and an English name, "The Healer."[78]

For Carlos, the highlight of the *Freedom* tour came on July 4, 1987, in Moscow, when Santana played before an enthusiastic crowd of more than 25,000 Russians. During the past several years, the reforming Soviet leader Mikhail Gorbachev had sought to improve relations between his country and the United States. Nonetheless, the Cold War between the two superpowers would not officially end until 1991 with the demise of Communist Party rule in Russia and the dissolution of the Soviet Union. Dismayed by the ongoing nuclear arms race between their two nations, 200 American and 200 Soviet citizens had staged a "Peace Walk" from Leningrad to Moscow during the summer of 1987, which was to culminate in the Soviet capital's giant soccer arena, Izmajlovo Stadium, on America's Independence Day. To commemorate the end of the

Peace Walk, Bill Graham had taken it upon himself to organize a free concert at the stadium. In addition to Santana, Graham had persuaded popular American musicians James Taylor, the Doobie Brothers, and Bonnie Rait as well as several Russian rock bands to perform.

Carlos was thrilled to be part of what he considered a noble cause, and the guitarist's impassioned performance at the Izmajlovo Stadium was a showstopper. "Basically, Santana commanded most of the admiration of the crowd," observed Russian rock singer Boris Grebenshikoz: "Carlos is something

LA BAMBA

In 1987, Carlos Santana was thrilled to have the opportunity to work with one of his favorite rock groups, the Los Angeles-based Latino band Los Lobos, in developing a soundtrack for *La Bamba*, a movie about the singer, songwriter, and guitarist, Ritchie Valens. Santana was particularly pleased to be part of the project because *La Bamba*'s script portrayed Mexicans in a positive light, something he believed Hollywood had failed to do in the past.

Ritchie Valens (born Richard Valenzuela) was the first Mexican-American rock star. Born in a suburb of Los Angeles on May 13, 1941, Ritchie was introduced to Mexican folk songs by his relatives when he was still a young child. During his junior year in high school, Valenzuela took up the electric guitar and joined the Silhouettes, a local rock and roll band. When record producer Bob Keane heard the band, he was immediately impressed by Ritchie and invited the teenager to audition for him. Ritchie signed with Keane's Del-Fi label in 1958 and released his first single, "Come On, Let's Go," under the name Ritchie Valens that same year. The record would eventually reach number 42 on the national charts. Ritchie's follow-up spiritual, he is so melodic and that is a sign of the spirit."[79] The Russians' enthusiastic response to Carlos Santana in the summer of 1987 made it clear that the 40-year-old guitarist was still revered as a musical superstar in some parts of the globe. Back in his home country, however, Santana worried that he was being viewed more and more as a throwback from the late 1960s and early 1970s—a relic from America's long-ago hippie era who had nothing to offer today's young listeners.

release, "Donna," a dreamy, slow-paced song that he had composed for his high school girlfriend, did even better, peaking at number 2.

Valens' next record, "La Bamba," was considerably more original than the sentimental "Donna." Sung entirely in Spanish, "La Bamba" was based on a Mexican folk song of the same name. Valens' lively version of the old ballad was a pioneering mixture of rock and roll and traditional Mexican music, and the song was an instant hit with the record-buying public and music critics alike.

During the winter of 1959, the 17-year-old performer embarked on a major tour of the Midwest with rock stars Buddy Holly and The Big Bopper (J.P. Richardson). On the night of February 2, the three musicians boarded a small, chartered airplane in Clear Lake, Iowa, bound for North Dakota. The plane crashed shortly after takeoff, killing everyone on board. Although Valens' recording career lasted for less than a year, his innovative blending of driving rock rhythms with Mexican folk music in "La Bamba" would have a significant impact on future generations of Latino rock musicians, including Carlos Santana.

7

Supernatural

The late 1980s was a trying time for Carlos Santana. After spending two decades with Columbia, he was feeling increasingly disgruntled with his record company. In the wake of a string of commercially unsuccessful albums, Columbia's top brass had all but given up on him, the guitarist suspected. In late 1987, Carlos released his sixth solo recording, the entirely instrumental, jazz fusion record *Blues for Salvador*. When *Blues for Salvador* only reached number 195 on the national charts, Santana blamed Columbia's executives for the album's meager sales, accusing them of making little effort to promote or market the record. Despite his disappointment with the album's sales, however, to Carlos' delight *Blues for Salvador* not only received glowing reviews in many jazz publications but also brought him his first ever Grammy Award when its title track was honored as the Best Rock Instrumental Performance of 1988.

A NEW RECORD LABEL

Carlos Santana's dissatisfaction with Columbia deepened following the release of his band's newest live album, *Viva Santana*, in late 1988. Carlos had been promised total creative freedom in assembling the anthology, which was to include live recordings from 1969 to the present. Nevertheless, the Columbia executives were clearly displeased when Carlos chose to ignore several of the band's hit songs from the 1970s and early 1980s in favor of less commercial, jazz- and fusion-oriented material. The record company's promotion of the new album was lukewarm at best and to Carlos' dismay, *Viva Santana* never made it beyond number 142 on the national album charts.

In 1990, Carlos began recording what was to be his final album with his band before their current contract with Columbia Records expired—*Spirits Dancing in the Flesh*. An energetic hodgepodge of soul, gospel, blues, Latin rock, and fusion, *Spirits Dancing in the Flesh* sold more copies than *Blues for Salvador*. Nonetheless, the record only reached number 85 on the national album charts. Carlos was more disillusioned with his record label than ever, blaming the album's mediocre showing in the charts on what he viewed as Columbia's half-hearted support for his music. In the wake of yet another marginal chart entry, he concluded that the time had come to end his long relationship with the record giant.

The following year, Carlos and his band signed a multi-album contract with Polygram Record's Polydor label. Carlos decided to throw in his lot with Polydor after the label's producers offered him total artistic freedom and the opportunity to create his own record label, Guts and Grace. Under the Guts and Grace label, Carlos planned to produce an anthology of never-before-released live material by several of his music idols, including the late John Coltrane, Jimi Hendrix, Jamaican reggae star Bob Marley, and guitarist Stevie Ray Vaughan. By making these rare live tracks from his private collection available to the record-buying public, Santana hoped to help preserve the artistic legacies of Coltrane and his other deceased heroes.

THREE NEW ALBUMS

Soon after signing with Polydor, Carlos began work on *Milagro* (Spanish for miracle), his first album with the Santana band for the new label. Released in 1992, the album was a blend of musical styles from around the globe, including reggae, soul, jazz, rock, and sensuous Afro-Cuban rhythms. Many of the tracks featured deeply spiritual and introspective lyrics that reflected Carlos' sorrow at the passing of two of his closest friends in late 1991: jazz legend Miles Davis, who died in September after suffering a stroke, and Bill Graham, who perished in a helicopter crash the following month. Although the album was only a modest seller, Carlos was heartened when *Milagro* received glowing reviews from several leading U.S. music publications, including *Rolling Stone*, which lauded it as "one of the finest sessions Santana has ever done. . . . His attack is razor sharp and his [guitar] solos rank among the best."[80]

In late 1993, Carlos released his second album under the Polydor label, *Sacred Fire*. Recorded earlier that year during the band's sold-out tour of Mexico, Argentina, and Venezuela and featuring the young rapper Vorriece Cooper, the live record included many of Santana's classic hits from the late 1960s and early 1970s, as well as new material. Carlos felt confident that the album would be a big seller. To his disappointment, however, like *Milagro*, *Sacred Fire* enjoyed only modest commercial success. Once again, Carlos placed the blame for his albums' mediocre sales squarely on his record label. Polydor, he believed, had let him down by failing to adequately promote his music. Soon after the release of *Sacred Fire*, Carlos resolved to leave Polydor for Island, another of Polygram's record labels.

Carlos' first major project for Island was a collaborative effort with two other talented Latin-American guitarists and composers: his younger brother Jorge, formerly of the popular Latin rock group Malo, and a 26-year-old nephew, Carlos

Hernandez. Although the all-instrumental album, which Santana dubbed *Brothers*, was only a moderate seller, it received positive reviews and was nominated for a Grammy Award for Best Rock Instrumental in 1994.

A DEVASTATING SECRET

By 1994, Carlos Santana was the doting father of three children: son Salvador, born in 1983, and daughters Stella and Angelica, born in 1985 and 1990, respectively. Yet, as much as he cherished his young family, Carlos was often withdrawn and ill-tempered during this period. The guitarist's recent professional disappointments clearly contributed to his moodiness: Carlos had placed high hopes in his new record company and was profoundly discouraged when his albums continued to sell poorly after he signed with Polygram. As her husband's irritability and depression grew during the mid-1990s, however, Deborah Santana became convinced that something more than his stagnating career was troubling Carlos. Finally, she gave her partner of more than 20 years an ultimatum. "I'm really worried and concerned because you have anger and more anger," Carlos remembered Deborah telling him: "I think you need to see a therapist to see what's going on with you, if you want to stay married with me."[81]

Convinced that his marriage was at stake, Carlos entered therapy in 1995. With his counselor's help, the guitarist was able to face his inner demons at last. After several months of intensive therapy, Carlos revealed something to his psychologist that he had never shared with another soul. When he was a young boy in Tijuana, he had been repeatedly molested by an American man who would drive the young street musician over the border into California several times a week. "I was seduced by toys, and I was seduced by being brought to America with all kinds of gifts and stuff," Carlos later reflected. "And, being a child, I blocked that other part, because there was the other goodies of somebody taking you to Sears and Roebuck."[82] Carlos finally ended the exploitative relationship when he turned 12 and fell in love with a girl for the first time. When the American caught Carlos staring at the girl, he became jealous and struck him viciously. "And I woke up," Santana remembered: "I looked at him for the first time for who he was: a very sick person."[83]

Carlos Santana had spent nearly four decades trying to block out the agonizing memories of his sexual abuse. "You want to get angry with yourself for not knowing better," he now says. "The mind has a very insidious way of making you feel guilty: You're the guilty party, shame on you, you're the one who brought this on yourself."[84] By courageously confronting the terrors of his childhood head-on, Carlos was able to make peace with his past: "I have learned to convert all this energy now into something productive and creative. Before I didn't have a way to express it and crystallize it and heal it. It's just fuel now. You use it to do something creative with. . . .Whether you are a woman or man who has been raped or molested, you don't have to ruin the rest of your life and ruin your family's life by blaming yourself, feeling dirty, ashamed," he told *Rolling Stone* magazine. "Burn all those things. . . . Put all those things in a letter, burn it, take the ashes, plant some roses and put the ashes on it, and watch it grow. And let it go."[85]

TALKING WITH ANGELS

Carlos' ability to heal from the pain he had suffered as a boy was due in large part to his strong spiritual beliefs. In addition to the months he spent in therapy, Santana credits his Christian heritage, meditation, and above all, a willingness to explore new spiritual directions, with helping him to overcome the pain and bitterness he had carried with him for nearly half a century.

About the time he started therapy, Carlos linked up with some fellow spiritual explorers in the Bay Area who were to have a significant impact not only on his personal life but also on his career. Carlos' new acquaintances were part of the so-called New Age movement. Founded during the late 1960s, the New Age movement draws on a wide range of spiritual and

By the mid-1990s, Carlos, pictured here with Deborah, had become involved in the New Age movement. The philosophy emphasizes an individual approach to spirituality and practitioners focus on spiritual and personal growth, psychological and physical healing, global peace, and harmony with the environment.

philosophical teachings, many of which have ancient roots. Its followers stress spiritual and personal growth, psychological and physical healing, global peace, and harmony with the environment. The fact that the loosely organized New Age movement has no formal doctrines, holy books, or clergy appealed to Carlos. "I like spirituality, not religion," he maintains. "Religion turns into 'My god's bigger than your god; therefore you're a heathen, and you should die, and I'll take your land and build a temple on top of your flattened house.' . . . Spirituality is not memorizing the Koran or the Bible while hurting people in the name of Allah or Jesus or Buddha or oil.

We are all chosen. Surely we have the capacity to transmute anger and fear into a masterpiece of joy."[86]

The New Age group that Santana became associated with during the mid-1990s was particularly interested in attaining personal enlightenment through channeling. Channeling is the ancient belief that individuals can communicate directly with angels and other benevolent spirits. During a meditation session, a member of the group informed Carlos that an angel named Metatron had given him an urgent message for the guitarist. Metatron wanted Santana to know that although nearly fifteen years had passed since he and his band had produced a hit record, their music would soon be back on the radio and more popular than ever.

According to Carlos, a few days later Metatron began speaking directly to him in his dreams and meditations. "We want to hook you back to the radio-airwave frequency," the angel told him. "We want you to reach junior high schools, high schools and universities. Once you reach them, . . . we want you to present them with a new menu. Let them know that they are themselves, multidimensional spirits with enormous possibilities and opportunities."[87] Whereas Carlos readily admits that this heavenly communiqué would probably strike most people as "very New Age and far out,"[88] to him Metatron's words made perfect sense. Carlos had long worried about the impact that the American media, with its emphasis on violence, escapism, and selfish materialism, was having on the younger generation. He believed that his music could provide America's youth with a more positive and uplifting message than they had been absorbing from movies, television, and much of the popular music of the day. If he could just get his songs back on radio, Carlos was convinced, his revitalized career would provide him with "an enormous capacity to be of service to people, especially young people, to let them know that they need to strengthen their aspirations and visions [and] . . . live up to their potential."[89]

"CREATE A MASTERPIECE OF JOY OUT OF YOUR LIFE"

In an interview conducted by author Bill Demain in 2003 for his book *In Their Own Words: Songwriters Talk about the Creative Process*, Carlos Santana explained how he views his life's work and the message of spiritual growth, hope, and compassion that he hopes to convey to his listeners through his music:

> I'm in to having fun, but also growing spiritually. Because I only have so much time while I'm visiting this planet. We come from the light, we're going to return to the light. I push beauty, elegance, excellence, grace, dignity. I don't push guilt, shame, judgment, condemnation, or fear. That's what rappers do a lot. I'd rather push beauty and purity and innocence. All of us have those things. You might misplace it but you never lose it. So *Shaman* and *Supernatural* are successful because we're touching on something that the Beatles used to do. "All You Need is Love," "Give Peace a Chance," "Imagine." Those songs are bigger than the Beatles now. Songs by Bob Marley are bigger than him now. Songs by John Coltrane are bigger than Coltrane now. That's what I want to be.*

In the same interview, the award-winning musician and philanthropist offered some heartfelt advice to aspiring musicians and artists and to young people in general:

> Everybody's capable of higher heights. Create a masterpiece of joy out of your life. Use your adversity and problems. Emotional this and that, use them as colors, use them as tools. We live in a freewill planet, but you are accountable and responsible for your choices. Those are big clues for people in junior high school and universities. You cannot behave appropriately unless you perceive correctly. So we are the light. Perceive that you are the light and then you will behave like that. You'll make a difference in the world.**

---

* Bill Demain, *In Their Own Words: Songwriters Talk about the Creative Process* (Westport, Conn.: Praeger, 2004), 75.
** Ibid., 73.

BACK IN THE PUBLIC EYE

Santana's conviction that angels were guiding him gave the guitarist a renewed sense of purpose. He became resolved to find a new record company, one that was prepared to give him the level of support necessary to get his music—and his message of hope and understanding—back on the airwaves and into the consciousness of America's young people.

Deborah Santana thought that she knew just the right person to help her husband recharge his faltering career. She urged Carlos to get back in touch with Clive Davis, Santana's long-ago mentor at Columbia during the late 1960s and early 1970s. Now the president of Arista Records, over the decades Davis had developed a reputation for turning out hit albums. At Deborah's urging, Carlos invited Davis to watch him and his band perform in New York City in 1997. After the concert, the guitarist and the record executive talked at length about Carlos' goals and dreams. Davis was deeply impressed by Santana's passion and determination. By the end of the year, Carlos had negotiated a contract with Arista and started drafting plans for a new album with his band.

The time certainly seemed ripe for Carlos Santana to make a comeback. Over the past several years, the American public and media had become increasingly infatuated with Latin-tinged music. By the late 1990s, the United States was in the midst of what some were dubbing a "Latin Explosion," as Hispanic singing sensations Jennifer Lopez, Ricky Martin, and Marc Anthony brought Latin pop to a larger and more diverse audience than ever before. In the midst of this Latin music renaissance, Carlos Santana found himself the focus of renewed media attention as one of the founders and chief icons of Latin rock.

In 1998, public interest in Carlos grew further when the guitarist and the Santana band were inducted into the Rock and Roll Hall of Fame. Few doubted that the recent Latin music boom had something to do with the timing of this highly publicized honor. Although Carlos had relied on a large and almost continuously evolving group of backing musicians ever since he took over the band in 1972, the Hall of Fame decided to induct only those six musicians who had performed at Woodstock in 1969 and recorded Santana's first two ground-breaking Latin-rock albums: Carlos Santana, Chepitó Areas, Gregg Rolie, Michael Shrieve, Michael Carabello, and David Brown.

A *SUPERNATURAL* PHENOMENON

Soon after being inducted into the Rock and Roll Hall of Fame, Carlos Santana began recording his first album for Clive Davis and Arista. At Davis' insistence, half of the album was to be classic Santana-style Latin rock in the spirit of "Black Magic Woman" and "Oye Como Va," and half was to consist of collaborations between Carlos and popular, young musicians who could help the guitarist appeal to a wider— and more youthful—audience than he had attracted in previous years. To that end, Davis recruited soul diva Lauryn Hill, Haitian-born rapper Wyclef Jean, Rob Thomas of the rock band Matchbox 20, and a host of other 1990s music sensations for Santana's newest project.

The album, which Carlos dubbed *Supernatural*, took nearly a year to record. When the CD was finally released in June 1999 amid heavy publicity, it was an almost instant hit. Although *Supernatural* barely squeaked into the Top 20 during its first week, it quickly began a steady ascent of the U.S. album charts and peaked at number 1. *Sacred Fire*, Carlos' previous album with the Santana band, had sold just 200,000 copies; *Supernatural* would eventually sell more than 15 million copies in the United States alone and 25 million worldwide, making the CD the best-selling album ever by a Latin-American artist. The album also spawned two number 1 songs: "Smooth," a catchy, salsa-tinged number featuring Rob Thomas, and the Latin-, African-, and Caribbean-influenced "Maria Maria," composed and produced by Wyclef Jean.

Carlos Santana (left) and Matchbox 20's Rob Thomas perform their song "Smooth" at the 2000 Grammy Awards. In addition to "Smooth" the album *Supernatural* spawned the number 1 hit "Maria Maria."

A MULTITUDE OF AWARDS

On February 23, 2000, *Supernatural*, which had received rave reviews in nearly all the leading American music publications, swept the 42nd Annual Grammy Awards. By the end of the evening, Carlos Santana had collected eight Grammy Awards, including the ceremony's most coveted honors, Album of the Year and Record of the Year (for "Smooth.") Only one other artist—Michael Jackson—had earned as many Grammys in a single year. At the first ever Latin Grammy Awards in Los Angeles in September 2000, Santana was once again the night's biggest winner, earning three awards, including Record of the Year for "Corazón Espinado," a song that he recorded for *Supernatural* with the Mexican supergroup Maná.

Two years later, Santana released his follow-up album to

Supernatural, Shaman. Coproduced by Clive Davis, *Shaman* stuck to the formula that had proven so successful for *Supernatural.* Approximately half of the CD featured Carlos and the Santana band performing their classic mixture of Latin, rock, blues, and jazz. The remainder of the album consisted of collaborations between the guitarist and a diverse troupe of young recording stars, including 19-year-old pop diva Michelle Branch, soul singer Macy Gray, pop sensation Seal, and Ozomatli, a multiethnic rock-Latin-soul group from East Los Angeles.

When the much-anticipated CD was released in October 2002, *Shaman* accomplished something no other Santana album had before—it debuted at number 1 on the Billboard 200 album chart. By November, the album had gone double platinum and spawned a number 1 single: "The Game of Love," featuring singer Michelle Branch. The following year, Santana and Branch earned a Grammy for Best Pop Collaboration with Vocals for the Latin- and R&B-laced song.

The awards kept pouring in for Carlos Santana during the early 2000s. In August 2004, Carlos was honored as the Latin Academy of Recording Arts and Sciences Person of the Year, and at the 12th annual BMI Latin Awards in April 2005, he was honored as a BMI Icon for his unique and enduring influence on American music. (The BMI is a performing rights organization that currently represents some 300,000 composers, songwriters, and music publishers in the United States.)

CARLOS SANTANA'S MISSION

By the beginning of the new millennium, Carlos Santana had attained wealth and fame beyond anything he had ever experienced in his nearly four-decade-long career. Yet Carlos had not lost sight of the spiritual values and goals that had spurred him to get his music and its message of hope and healing back on the radio in the first place. Consequently, he was thrilled to learn that *Supernatural* had expanded his fan base to encompass Americans of all ages, including millions of teenagers who had

(continued on page 104)

MEXICAN MUSIC'S INFLUENCE ON CARLOS SANTANA

In the wake of the extraordinary commercial success of *Supernatural*, Santana frequently found himself being lauded in the press as a Mexican or Latino icon. It was a label that he strongly resisted. "There's only one truth in this planet and that is that we are all one," he told Jesse Varela of *Latin Beat* magazine soon after the album began climbing the charts during the summer of 1999: "The opposite of truth is illusion. It is your choice if you just want to be a Chicano living around four blocks in the Mission [District] but that is not who you are completely. You and I are multidimensional spirits with tremendous opportunities and possibilities. It's your choice. I woke up a long time ago and realized that I am the whole rainbow."

Throughout his long recording and performing career, Carlos Santana has often seemed to go out of his way to downplay his ethnic and national origins: "I'm an Earth citizen. I feel I can relate to kids in Hong Kong as well as Tijuana. Being Mexican is not all I am. I am Hebrew, I am Palestinian, I am everything. I can grasp the absolute- ness. I can go to Africa or Cuba or Brazil or Geneva and can be part of the family, not just a tourist," he informed Edna Gunderson of *USA Today* in 2002. "Everyone knows that I don't wrap myself with any enchilada," he declared in an interview with *Billboard* magazine two years later: "I don't like flags. I really don't. I respect that some people like that, but that's a dinosaur existence. To me, the only flag is a man, a woman and a child. That's the only flag I pledge allegiance to."

Santana is clearly convinced that humankind's spiritual, cultural, and social advancement depends on a willingness to overlook tradition- al boundaries, whether they are racial, religious, or ethnic divisions; national borders; or musical genres. In truth, however, the guitarist- songwriter's own work and life have been significantly impacted by his Mexican roots. As a musician, Carlos Santana has always drawn from an exceptionally diverse palette, ranging from the Delta blues of Muddy Waters to the African rhythms of Nigerian drummer Babatunde Olatunji to the cutting-edge jazz fusion of Miles Davis. Nevertheless, Hispanic—and particularly Mexican—influences have played a critical role in molding his music and career.

Santana's Hispanic heritage is not only apparent in his heavy reliance on classic Afro-Cuban rhythms and percussion in his music. Carlos' distinctive guitar style also owes a great deal to the musical legacy of his land of birth. As Santana's biographer Simon Leng has pointed out, expert mariachi violinists like Carlos' own father, José Santana, are known for their ability to create a wistful, almost pleading tone on their instruments by holding the same note for a very long time. By the time his career was beginning to take off in the mid-1960s, Carlos Santana had adopted the sustained concept that has long been an integral feature of Mexican folk music in his own playing. Indeed, Santana's penchant for sustaining extraordinarily long, searing notes on his guitar is generally considered his trademark as a musician.

Another characteristically Mexican quality of Carlos' guitar technique is his richly melodic and emotional style of playing. Once again, Leng gives Carlos' mariachi violinist father José the primary credit for teaching Santana how to play music—whether rock and roll, blues, jazz, or fusion—with a distinctly Mexican accent. José not only taught Carlos the long, flowing melodies of the traditional Mexican sones and folk ballads, he also drilled into his son the importance of imbuing every note with as much expression—or *duende* (soul) in Mexican—as possible. By observing his musician father at work in his hometown of Autlán de Navarro, Carlos learned from a very early age that music, when played with true duende, could be much more than mere entertainment: it could be a means of connecting people with their innate spirituality and deepest emotions. Like his unique and much-lauded guitar style, Santana's lifelong faith in the power of music to heal, inspire, and stir both the heart and the soul is firmly rooted in Mexican traditions and values.

In 1998, Carlos and Deborah Santana established the Milagro Foundation, a nonprofit group dedicated to assisting underprivileged children throughout the world. Deborah is pictured here at the Milagro Foundation Benefit fashion show and silent auction in 2004, which was held in support of the Violence Intervention Program of Los Angeles.

(*continued from page 101*)

never even heard of Santana before the CD's release in 1999. "I receive web postings from people saying over and over, 'Because of *Supernatural*, I made a connection with my teenager who I haven't talked to in a long time, even though we live in the same house and we drive in the same car,'" Santana proudly told a reporter: "All of a sudden, music has the capacity to break that gap—'Hey, Dad, turn that up.' I'm really honored to be a part of bringing a gentler form of communication between a father and a son or a mother and a daughter. The fabric of family is something that's been shattered in America. This is why we're infected with fear and anger on every channel of TV and radio."[90]

The phenomenal success of the *Supernatural* and *Shaman* albums has also given Carlos the opportunity to provide more financial support than ever before to a host of charitable and social causes. From the earliest years of his recording career, Santana had been one of the music world's leading philanthropists, participating in benefit concerts for Live Aid, which donated millions of dollars to African famine victims in 1985, Amnesty International, and countless other charitable endeavors during the 1970s and 1980s. In 1998, he and Deborah founded the nonprofit Milagro Foundation, dedicated to assisting underprivileged children and youth around the globe through grants to agencies and charities involved in health, education, and the arts. Among the many different organizations that Milagro supports are two that provide counseling to children who have suffered sexual abuse, a cause close to Carlos' heart.

In 2003, Milagro distributed approximately a quarter of a million dollars to more than 50 organizations worldwide. The Milagro Foundation is funded almost entirely by Carlos himself, with a portion of every record and every concert ticket he sells going directly to the organization. A percentage of Santana's proceeds from the Brown Shoe Company's Carlos Santana footwear line, which debuted in 2000, also goes to the foundation.

"I believe it's important to do something you love," declares Carlos Santana. "We all have a part to play in making this a better world, whether it's uniting people through music, which is what I try to do, being good parents, or working in our communities. We also need to give back from whatever success we've been blessed to have. Success isn't about being top on the charts or having a lot of money. It's about being good at whatever you do and finding a way to help other people along the way."[91]

Chronology and Timeline

1947 Born in Autlán de Navarro, Mexico, on July 20.

1955 Moves to the border town of Tijuana, Mexico.

1963 Settles in the Mission District of San Francisco, California, with his family.

1966 Helps found the Santana Blues Band, which later becomes simply Santana.

1968 The Santana band headlines at the Fillmore West Auditorium in San Francisco.

1969 Santana gains a national audience at the Woodstock Art and Music Fair and the band releases its first album, *Santana*.

1970 *Abraxas*, the second Santana album, climbs to the top of the album charts.

1947
Born in Autlán de Navarro, Mexico, on July 20

1963
Settles in the Mission District of San Francisco, California, with his family

1969
Santana gains a national audience at the Woodstock Music Fair and the band releases its first album, *Santana*

1947

1972

1955
Moves to the border town of Tijuana, Mexico

1972
Original Woodstock-era Santana band breaks up

1966
Helps found the Santana Blues Band

1971 *Santana III* is released.

1972 Original Woodstock-era Santana band breaks up; Carlos moves toward jazz fusion in the album *Caravanserai* and becomes a disciple of Indian guru Sri Chinmoy.

1973 Carlos marries Deborah King in April.

1977 "She's Not There" from the double album *Moonflower* becomes Santana's first Top-40 single in five years.

1981 Carlos and Deborah break with Sri Chinmoy.

1982 The single "Hold On" from the album *Shango* hits the Top 40.

1983 Carlos' and Deborah's first child, Salvador, is born.

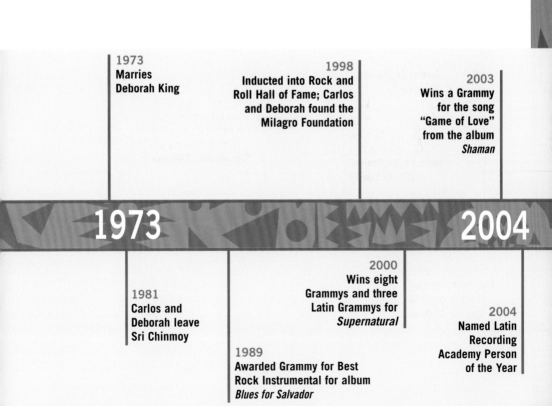

1973
Marries
Deborah King

1998
Inducted into Rock and
Roll Hall of Fame; Carlos
and Deborah found the
Milagro Foundation

2003
Wins a Grammy
for the song
"Game of Love"
from the album
Shaman

1973

2004

1981
Carlos and
Deborah leave
Sri Chinmoy

2000
Wins eight
Grammys and three
Latin Grammys for
Supernatural

2004
Named Latin
Recording
Academy Person
of the Year

1989
Awarded Grammy for Best
Rock Instrumental for album
Blues for Salvador

1989   Carlos is awarded the Grammy for Best Rock Instrumental of 1988 for the album *Blues for Salvador*.

1998   The Woodstock-era lineup of the band Santana is inducted into Rock and Roll Hall of Fame; Carlos and Deborah found the Milagro Foundation.

1999   Album *Supernatural* is released and quickly becomes a best-seller.

2000   Carlos wins eight Grammys and three Latin Grammys for best-selling album *Supernatural*.

2002   Album *Shaman* is released and quickly climbs to the top of the charts.

2003   Santana and Michelle Branch win a Grammy for their song, "Game of Love."

2004   Carlos is named Latin Recording Academy Person of the Year.

2005   Carlos is honored as an Icon at BMI Latin Awards.

Notes

Chapter 1

1 Leila Cobo, "Carlos Santana: The Altruistic Superstar," *Hispanic*, December 2004, 36.

2 Adam Sweeting, "Return of the Hippie," *The Manchester Guardian*, February 10, 2000.

3 Cobo, "Carlos Santana: The Altruistic Superstar," 36.

Chapter 2

4 "Santana," San Francisco Mission District, *www.sfmission.com/Santana*.

5 Chris Heath, "The Epic Life of Carlos Santana," *Rolling Stone*, March 16, 2000, 43.

6 Timothy White, "A Portrait of the Artist," *Billboard*, December 7, 1996, 14.

7 Marc Shapiro, *Back on Top: Carlos Santana* (New York: St. Martin's Press, 2000), 17.

8 Heath, "The Epic Life of Carlos Santana," 43.

9 White, "A Portrait of the Artist," 15.

10 Ibid.

11 Steve Heilig, "Carlos Santana," *Whole Earth*, Summer 2000, 73.

12 White, "A Portrait of the Artist," 15.

13 Heilig, "Carlos Santana," 73.

14 White, "A Portrait of the Artist," 15.

15 Heath, "The Epic Life of Carlos Santana," 43.

16 Shapiro, *Back on Top*, 26.

17 Simon Leng, *Soul Sacrifice: The Santana Story* (London: Fire Fly, 2000), 16.

18 Shapiro, *Back on Top*, 26–27.

19 Ibid., 27.

Chapter 3

20 White, "A Portrait of the Artist," 15.

21 John Tobler and Stuart Grundy, *The Guitar Greats* (New York: St. Martin's Press, 1984), 145.

22 Heilig, "Carlos Santana," 73.

23 Ibid., 74.

24 Shapiro, *Back on Top*, 50.

25 White, "A Portrait of the Artist," 15.

26 Marlo Thomas, ed., *The Right Words at the Right Time* (New York: Atria Books, 2002), 304.

27 White, "A Portrait of the Artist," 16.

28 Ibid., 15.

29 Shapiro, *Back on Top*, 53.

30 Tom Wheeler, "Encore," *Guitar Player*, July 2003, 25.

31 White, "A Portrait of the Artist," 16.

32 Heilig, "Carlos Santana," 74.

33 White, "A Portrait of the Artist," 16.

34 Shapiro, *Back on Top*, 38.

35 Heath, "The Epic Life of Carlos Santana," 44.

36 White, "A Portrait of the Artist," 16.

37 Tobler and Grundy, *The Guitar Greats*, 145.

38 Heath, "The Epic Life of Carlos Santana," 44.

39 White, "A Portrait of the Artist," 16.

Chapter 4

40 Shapiro, *Back on Top*, 47.

41 Edward J. Rielly, *The 1960s* (Westport, Conn.: Greenwood Press, 2003), 166.

42 Bill Graham and Robert Greenfield, *Bill Graham Presents: My Life inside Rock and Out* (New York: Doubleday, 1992), 211.

43 Ibid., 212.

44 Heilig, "Carlos Santana," 74.

45 Graham and Greenfield, *Bill Graham Presents*, 211.

46 "Carlos Santana on Recruiting Minority Teachers," *NEA Today*, May 2000, 21.

47 Ibid.

48 Thomas, ed., *The Right Words at the Right Time*, 304–05.

49 Graham and Greenfield, *Bill Graham Presents*, 213.

50 Ibid.

51 Heilig, "Carlos Santana," 75.

52 Graham and Greenfield, *Bill Graham Presents*, 213.

53 White, "A Portrait of the Artist," 17.

54 Thomas, ed., *The Right Words at the Right Time*, 306.

55 White, "A Portrait of the Artist," 17.

56 Ibid.

Chapter 5

57 Heilig, "Carlos Santana," 75.

58 Heath, "The Epic Life of Carlos Santana," 45.

59 Graham and Greenfield, *Bill Graham Presents*, 284.

60 Heath, "The Epic Life of Carlos Santana," 45.

61 Barry Hoskyns, *Beneath the Diamond Sky: Haight-Ashbury, 1965–1970* (New York: Simon & Schuster, 1997), 195.

62 Graham and Greenfield, *Bill Graham Presents*, 286.

63 Leng, *Soul Sacrifice*, 59.

64 Shapiro, *Back on Top*, 119.

65 Ibid., 96.

66 Ibid., 125.

67 Joel Selvin, *Summer of Love: The Inside Story of LSD, Rock & Roll, Free Love and High Times in the Wild West* (New York: Dutton, 1994), 327.

68 Leng, *Soul Sacrifice*, 66.

Chapter 6

69 White, "A Portrait of the Artist," 17.

70 Ibid.

71 Shapiro, *Back on Top*, 122–23.

72 Heath, "The Epic Life of Carlos Santana," 46.

73 Tobler and Grundy, *The Guitar Greats*, 150.

74 Ibid., 151–52.

75 Deborah Santana, *Space Between the Stars: My Journey to an Open Heart* (New York: Ballantine Books, 2005), 257.

76 Ibid., 261–62.

77 Ibid., 262.

78 Leng, *Soul Sacrifice*, 142.

79 Ibid., 143–44.

Chapter 7

80 Shapiro, *Back on Top*, 200.

81 Heath, "The Epic Life of Carlos Santana," 47.

82 Ibid.

83 Ibid.

84 Ibid., 48.

85 Ibid.

86 Edna Gunderson, "Spirit of Santana," *USA Today*, October 16, 2002.

87 David Wild, "Cosmic Carlos," *Rolling Stone*, August 19, 1999, 48.

88 Wild, "Cosmic Carlos," 48.

89 Chuy Varela, "Santana: In the Open," *Hispanic*, May 2000, 82.

90 G. Brown, "Heart and Soul: Carlos Santana Speaks Out on 'Shallow' Latin Pop," *Denver Post*, July 8, 2003.

91 "Carlos Santana on Recruiting Minority Teachers," 21.

Bibliography

Books

Demain, Bill. *In Their Own Words: Songwriters Talk about the Creative Process*. Westport, Conn.: Praeger, 2004.

Graham, Bill, and Robert Greenfield. *Bill Graham Presents: My Life inside Rock and Out*. New York: Doubleday, 1992.

Hoskyns, Barney. *Beneath the Diamond Sky: Haight-Ashbury, 1965–1970*. New York: Simon & Schuster, 1997.

Leng, Simon. *Soul Sacrifice: The Santana Story*. London: Fire Fly Publishers, 2000.

Rielly, Edward J. *The 1960s*. Westport, Conn.: Greenwood Press, 2003.

Santana, Deborah. *Space Between the Stars: My Journey to an Open Heart*. New York: Ballantine Books, 2005.

Selvin, Joel. *Summer of Love: The Inside Story of LSD, Rock & Roll, Free Love and High Times in the Wild West*. New York: Dutton, 1994.

Shapiro, Marc. *Back on Top: Carlos Santana*. New York: St. Martin's Press, 2000.

Thomas, Marlo, ed. *The Right Words at the Right Time*. New York: Atria Books, 2002.

Tobler, John, and Stuart Grundy. *The Guitar Greats*. New York: St. Martin's Press, 1984.

Periodicals

Brown, G. "Heart and Soul: Carlos Santana Speaks Out on 'Shallow' Latin Pop." *Denver Post*, July 8, 2003.

"Carlos Santana on Recruiting Minority Teachers." *NEA Today*, May 2000, 21.

Cobo, Leila. "Carlos Santana: The Altruistic Superstar." *Hispanic*, December 2004, 36–39.

———. "Santana." *Billboard*, August 14, 2004, 21–26.

Garza, Henry. "Carlos Santana." *Rolling Stone*, April 21, 2005, 98.

Gates, David, and Devin Gordon. "Smooth as Santana." *Newsweek*, February 14, 2000, 66–67.

Gunderson, Edna. "Spirit of Santana." *USA Today*, October 16, 2002.

Heath, Chris. "The Epic Life of Carlos Santana." *Rolling Stone*, March 16, 2000, 38–48.

Heilig, Steve. "Carlos Santana." *Whole Earth*, Summer 2000, 72–77.

Menard, Valerie. "The Man Behind the Music." *Hispanic*, March 1996, 18–21.

Selvin, Joel. "Carlos Santana: Still with the Good Fight." *San Francisco Chronicle*, August 17, 1986.

Sweeting, Adam. "Return of the Hippie." *The Manchester Guardian*, February 10, 2000.

Varela, Chuy. "Santana: In the Open." *Hispanic*, May 2000, 82.

Varela, Jesse. "Carlos Santana, Guitarrista." *Latin Beat*, September 1999, 9.

Wheeler, Tom. "Encore." *Guitar Player*, July 2003, 25.

White, Timothy. "A Portrait of the Artist." *Billboard*, December 7, 1996, 14–17.

Wild, David. "Cosmic Carlos." *Rolling Stone*, August 19, 1999, 47–49.

Web sites

Carlos Santana Official Site
www.santana.com

San Francisco Mission District: Santana
www.sfmission.com/santana

Web sites

Milagro Foundation
www.milagrofoundation.org

MTV Profile
http://www.mtv.com/bands/az/santana/artist.jhtml

Rock and Roll Hall of Fame Profile
http://www.rockhall.com/hof/inductee.asp?id=184

Carlos Santana Official Site
www.santana.com

San Francisco Mission District: Santana
www.sfmission.com/santana

Further Reading

Books and Periodicals

Cobo, Leila. "Carlos Santana: The Altruistic Superstar." *Hispanic*, December 2004, 36–39.

Leng, Simon. *Soul Sacrifice: The Santana Story*. London: Fire Fly Publishers, 2000.

Shapiro, Marc. *Back on Top: Carlos Santana*. New York: St. Martin's Press, 2000.

Tobler, John, and Stuart Grundy. *The Guitar Greats*. New York: St. Martin's Press, 1984.

Index

Picture Credits

About the Author

Louise Chipley Slavicek received her master's degree in history from the University of Connecticut. She has written 12 other books for young people, including *The Great Wall of China* and *Abraham Lincoln*. She lives in Ohio with her husband, James, a research biologist, and their children, Krista and Nathan.